Okinawa Diet

The longevity Diet

Table of Contents

CONTENTS

DEDICATION

The immortals kept their mental energies focused and refined,and harmonized their bodies with the environment.

Thus, they did not show conventional signs of aging and were able to live beyond biological limitations.

————

Yellow   Emperor's   Classic   of   Medicine

FOREWARD

Eternal youth

Eternal youth is a myth mentioned in legends and biblical stories. The issue of longevity has long been connected to religion since ancient times.

The famous patriarch Methuselah died at the age of 969 years, so the oldest person in the Bible become asynonym for longevity.

The reason could be explained in the respect of the human body as a temple of the holy spirit.

The longevity still remained with Noah who died at 950 years. Ashkenazi lineage may possess his longevitygenes.Ashkenaz is the first son of Gomer,son of Japhet,son of Noah.

Hippocrates believed in "the healing power of nature",or Vis medicatrix naturae.It was through the Jewish physician that much of the ancient Greek medical knowledge was preserved.

The Greek Pedanios compiled "Materia medica" which recognized almost 500 plants for medical treatment.

Ancient Egyptians were familiar with herbs,mostly due to the extensive mummification ceremonies.

The Edwin Smith Papyrus is medical textbook on herbal treatment involved at improvement of longevity.

The use of medical herbs was popular during the age of the Silk Road from the East to the West. Taoists lived a long time through the alchemy of herbs to bring about physical changes within the body.

Taoism focused on the the idea of living in harmony with nature.Health can only be achieved when the microcosm, (represented in every person) is in balance with the macrocosm or universe.

Shambala(Sanskrit:happiness) is a core concept in Tibetan Buddhism that describes a realm of harmony between man and nature where sages live immortality.

The Benedictine Hildegard of Bingen believed in the harmony between man and nature. The balance is the virtuous path of moderation through the health lifestyle.

Unlike the previously mentioned philosophy,the alchemist Paracelsus also believed in the idea of harmony.

The health relied on the harmony of Man(microcosm) and Nature(macrocosm).

Modern toxicology was influenced by his chemical remedies that can be found in medical herbs.

Many believe that successful aging is linked to an increase of good regular exercises and health habits.

Benjamin Franklin's writings exerted greatest influence in the medical world.His Poor Richard's Almanac promoted his thoughts in health benefits of exercises and moderate diet for extending lifespan.

––––––––––

There is evidence that the "Blue Zones" have higher numbers of centenarians.

They indicates limited regions, since demographers drew concentric blue circles to the health zones in Sardinia.

––––––––––

There are several geographic areas where populations live healthier and longest:Nicoya in Costa Rica,Okinawa in Japan,Loma Linda in California,Sardinia in Italy.

Scientists have been trying for years to discover the secrets of longevity.

The Akea Study (sardinian:centenarian) hypothesized that there may be genetic factors influencing Sardinian longevity.

Scientists argue that the environmental and lifestyle may help to improve the aging process of the older population.

Centenarians of Blue Zones shares a common lifestyle and environment:

1.they have low caloric intake from ancestral diet

2.they live included in family life and in the community

3.the religiosity is associated with health habits

4.the daily routine is based on low physical activity

Despite the interest towards longevity,the pressures of modern life may shorten the lifespan prematurely.

People subjected to stress tend to have telomere shortening in the cells.Telomeres are tiny caps that tip the ends of chromosomes.

For example,longer telomeres are the "secret to longevity" in Amish population who have been genetically and culturally isolated.Lifestyle may affect telomere length.

Japanese government has honoured centenarians with a silver sake cup and a congratulatory letter from the prime minister.

Japan has the highest percentage of centenarians anywhere according to data from the World Health Organization.

––––––––––

Okinawa Prefecture is well known as "the Longevity Island" for its elders with low levels of stress experienced.

This was possible only because of the ecological wisdom perpetuated in its way of life within the Okinawan culture.

The natural diet and and lifestyle make up the elixir for a better way of living.

CHAPTER 1

The country of courtesy

Okinawa Island (Okinawan:Uchinaa,rope) is a prefecture of Japan,located in the the Ryukyu archipelago,surrounded by the China Sea and the Pacific Ocean.

Anthropological studies revealed that the Ryukyuan people and the Ainu of Hokkaido share similar genetic traits despite living on opposite ends of the Japan.

The first king of Okinawa,Shunten (13th century) placed emphasis on military matters, and during his rule the Aji lords lived in castles (Gusuku) in their respective areas of influence.

Okinawa was divided into three Three Kingdoms: the south, called Nanzan,the central area, called Chuzan, and the north, called Hokuzan.

The Japanese imperial state had much exchange with China in the Taika Era.Taira clan had very close ties with Imperial China and carried knowledge of economic relations in Okinawa.

According to the Veritable Records of the Ming Dynasty,the Chinese Imperial government sent envoys to the "country of courtesy" in 1372.Being at the crossroads of major sea routes,Okinawa prospered economically as a center for intermediary trade in the Pacific region.

By the 15th century, the First Ryukyu Dynasty was founded by King Sho Hashi who unified the Ryukyu Kingdom.

The Ryukyus welcomed "36 Clans of the Min-People" from Fujian Province.

The chinese community was established in Kume village in the harbor of Naha,the port city of Okinawa.

The royal court recognized the potential role of chinese culture and confucian practices were encouraged into many aspects of life.

Later, the King Sho Shin centralized the Ryūkyū Kingdom by forcing local Aji lords to live at Shuri castle.The Shuri dialect became the official language of the country. He confiscated weapons to lower the possibility of rebellion.

Additionally,the Shuri court provided government positions to the Yukatchu class(chinese).This period was also called the Golden Age of the Ryukyus.

By 1600 the the Tokugawa shogunate authorized Satsuma domain to conquer the Ryūkyū Kingdom.In 1611,the Shimazu clan from Kyushu promulgated the "Fifteen Articles" to rule over Okinawa as a vassal state.

Satsuma took take advantage of Ryūkyū's trade with China soon,so Ryukyuans made great efforts in keeping the invasion a secret from the Chinese.

In 1854,Commodore Perry forced Tokugawa Shogun to sign the "Convention of Kanagawa" for the opening of trade relations between and the United States. In the same perod,the Kingdom of the Ryūkyūs signed the "Treaty of Peace and Amity".

In 1875,the kingdom was replaced by Okinawa Prefecture while China's relationship with the islands was abolished in 1879.

The Meiji government formulated imperial policy contained in the edict entitled the "Disposition of the Ryukyus".

The Okinawan culture has gone through the process of assimilation into Japanese Emperor.

The Uchinanchu diaspora was a large wave of emigration abrod at the end of the 19th century.

The Okinawan people occupied the low end of the economic scale in Japan.

Poverty prevailed in agricultural villages and people migrated abroad.The situation was also aggravated by natural disasters such as typhoons and droughts.

The Uchinanchu communities preserved essential aspects of ancestral culture, establishing the Uchinanchu Network abroad.

Iha Fuyū was the father of Okinawaology and his famous book,Old Ryūkyū, was one of the best works on Okinawan studies.The scholar devoted much time in preserving ancient Okinawan culture.

Today, the World Uchinanchu Festival plays a central role to passing down Uchinanchu identity to the next generations.

Unfortunately, the Ryūkyūs lost the peace with the battle of Okinawa ,at the end of World War II.

On April 1, 1945 US troops landed on Okinawa's beaches (Operation Iceberg) to start the invasion of Japan.

Okinawa Memorial Day is a public holiday observed in Japan's Okinawa Prefecture annually on June 23 to remember civilian population died. Approximately, 240,000 people, including the civilian population were killed.

After World War II,Okinawa was under United States Military Government of the Ryūkyū Islands which began land expropriations in support of the strengthening of the U.S. Navy bases in order to promote stability in East Asia.

The native Kariyushi (Okinawan:harmony with nature) movement for self-determination continue to seek the removal of military bases.

Okinawa remained under the control of the United States for 27 years until it was finally returned to Japan in 1972.

The Japanese government signed the Okinawa Reversion Agreement to Japan sovereignity with the United States.

Expo '75 World's Fair commemorates the American handover of Okinawa to Japan in 1972.

The motto "The sea we would like to see" was envisioned as a concept of how humans could live in harmony with nature.

Fujian province is pursuing a bigger role in the international trade routes namely the 21st Century Maritime Silk Road.

Okinawa had to deal with the coming challenges in Eastern China.

Okinawa Prefecture and Fujian province together planted a tree in Fuzhou,by rediscovering their ancient spirit of friendship.

The sister relationship will bring economical benefits to the two peoples.

The Hidari-Gomon symbol was adopted as the official government symbol to Okinawa Prefecture. The white circle symbolizes peace and the inner circle symbolizes a globally developing Okinawa.

In the 21st century, Okinawa should eventually become a "bridge between nations"(Bankoku Shinryo) and a Crossroad of Peace in the Asia Pacific Region.

CHAPTER 2

The Land of the immortals

Emperor Jimmu was the first Emperor of the Yamato dynasty who died when he was 126 years old, according to the japanese mythology of "Kojiki".

Japan instituted a strict record keeping system and census policy in the 1870s: the registry system of birth (koseki)verified the longevity of population.

Japan possess the the longest life expectancy in the world.Japanese centenarians receive a certificate from the Prime Minister of Japan,honouring them for their longevity.

Ancient Chinese legends already called Okinawa "the land of the immortals", the first place in Japan where life span is above 100 years.

The remote Ogimi village of Okinawa has achieved the title of "longevity village" for its high number of centenarians. They have a lower risk of heart attack and stroke, cancer, osteoporosis and Alzheimer.

Japan Ministry of Health and Welfare founded Okinawan Centenarian Study gerontologist in order to study health benefits of Okinawan style of life.

Medical studies postulated that OKinawans come from an island population with high DHEA levels in the blood,a steroid that prevent the risk of age-diseases.

Generally,persons with higher levels of DHEAS production tend to live longer.DHEA can become essential for body's anti-aging defenses.

They have also identified a single gene,APOE, absent in the centenarians.APOE is a genetic variant believed to increase the risk for developing Alzheimer's disease.

Aging is associated with a decline of physiological functions that can affect nutritional status.

Older adults often have reduced appetite with the decline in the ability to absorb essential nutrients.

The diet is an extremely important factor with anti-inflammatory compounds which help prevent the risk of in chronic diseases.

Research suggests that centenarians have high levels of vitamin A-D-E and that nutrients seems to be associated with longevity.

Okinawan culture is a model of balanced diet which maximizes the consumption of locally natural ingredients.

The daily diet is based intake of essential nutrients (antioxidants)which are extremely important to reducing the formation of free radicals.

Free radicals are the principal factors behind almost every known disease according to some researchers.

OKinawa seem to appear also to be area with low caloric density diet.

Generally, the term "calorie restriction" refers to dietary regimens that reduce calorie intake from a poor diet.

Around 1500 the Venetian nobleman Luigi Cornaro adopted a calorie restricted diet and became centenarian.

Cornaro revealed the secret of longevity in his book:"The Sure and Certain Method of Attaining a Long and Healthful Life".

The Venetian nobleman suggested the principle of calorie restriction in his personal diet.

Clive McCay was author of the first publication on calorie restriction:"The Effect of Retarded Growth upon the Length of Life Span and upon the Ultimate Body Size".

This early study have shown that calorie restriction intake without malnutrition may indirectly slow the aging process in humans.

Since ancient time, poverty rate in Okinawa have been consistently high which makes the Japanese prefecture one of the poorest areas in the country.It is believed that lower calorie intake is a major contributor to their remarkable longevity.

The philosophy of Confucius is reflected in food culture among communities of Okinawans.

"Hara hachi bu" is a Confucian teaching that advises people to eat slowly until they are approximately 80 percent full.

By following these principles Okinawans eat small portions and they are less hungry.

The sociologist Émile Durkheim in his Division of Labour in Society argued that collective "consciousness" is the totality of social norms within a social group.

The contents of individual's consciousness are shared in common with the social environment, making feel connected to the community.

All traditional societies originated from agricultural values of times.

––––––––––

The community developed with the founding clan settled in each okinawan village was at the center of familial aspects of communal life.

The traditional culture still exists through local institutions:

a)Yuimaru(circle) is a form of group work where farmers receive reciprocal support with the planting and harvesting of crops without being paid.

b)Moai is an informal group for sustaining the village where members get finalcial support for their business.

Centenarians have been able to take advantage from rural society.By practicing the mutual aid, olders never feel isolated.

The Okinawan society is characterized by a strong sense of comunity,also known as "Ikigai" or in short words the purpose in life.

Elderly Okinawans feel valued, respected and kept as an integral part of the community.They have an active role in the family after retirement to be considered "living treasures" or mentors.

Many of the diseases suffered by older persons are the result of changes that naturally occur with the ageing process.

Okinawans have a positive attitude toward life. They enjoy each moment that make one's life worthwhile for aging successfully.

The influence of Buddhism religion reminds them the fleeting nature of the human beings.The religious belief puts cultivation of calm state of mind in first place.

The secret of longevity lies in the plentiful wisdom of okinawan ancestors which is inherited at present.

CHAPTER 3

The mandate of Heaven

Spiritual Health is one of four dimensions to well-being as defined by the World Health Organization(WHO),which include physical,social and mental.

People of Okinawa live in harmony with nature and local shrines are natural places.The Ryūkyūs Shinto is the indigenous belief devoted to the the respecting of Kami,divine spirits inhabiting rocks,trees,caves and springs.

The worship of ancestry originated from Utaki,sacred grove for the worship of gods.

The clans of the villages are mediators in relation to the deity with rituals and ceremonies to ensure prosperity.

The King was considered the axle between the Heaven and the Earth in charge of an harmonious society.

The idea of benevolent monarch was influenced particularly by China,which extended cultural hegemony over Ryūkyūs.

Chinese records described the political power of the spiritual power of the founder clan or Nebito, and his sister, the Negami or foundress,symbolism of the male female principal of the universe, like Yin and Yang.

The "onarigami" belief placed strong emphasis upon the role of the "kami-sisters".

The Ryūkyū kingdom established the office of High Priestess "Kikoe-Ogimi" to protect the King and its dynasty.

The "priestesses" (noro) gave prayers at the Utaki, the natural altar where Kami descend to listen to the sacred songs. The Omoro Soshi is the primary source of the traditional shaman rituals.

––––––––––

On the other hand,the "kaminchu" is a shaman with the ability to communicate direct the power of kami. Additionally,they are in charge of the religious rites against misfortune in each village in Ryūkyūs.

Even today, Confucian values are an integral part of okinawan culture including worshipping one's ancestors.

The ceremonies are led by the elder women who pass on family traditions in the household as well as performing rituals.

More important is the veneration of ancestors who are not seen as separate from the community.

Ancestral spirits are believed to reside in the memorial woods(ihai) which are placed on the top of the "buchidan" family altar.

The "Shimisai" is the annual tradition where families gather around family tombs for food and prayers offering to antenates.

There are older women called "Yuta" who intercede on humans through a trance state with their ancestor.

Yuta performed exorcism to separate a deceased person's soul (mabui), from the living family members.

According to Buddhist ethics,merits was the protective energy used with regard to ancestor worship.

Transferring merit to one's deceased relatives has become part of rituals and festivals. Virtuous lifestyle determines the quality of the next life in a family of good lineage.

––––––––––

The core of the ancestral worship is the "Bon celebration" which revitalizes the spirit of the community for three days of the lunar calendar.

Young dancers of the villages perform the famous "Eisa dance" all the night.The "Chunjun Nagari" song from Pure Land Buddism honours antenates passed away.

––––––––––

Kumi odori was the traditional dance created originally as part of formal court entertainments to welcome Chinese envoys.Okinawa has a long tradition of dance imported from Fujian.

Kumi odori was named an "important intangible cultural asset"by the Japanese government and named an "Intangible Cultural Heritage" of the world by UNESCO.

Annual festivals conclude with popular Kacha-si dance by hand(wrist) movements.Dancers wear the colorful "Bingata kimono" of printed cotton from China.

Studies has confirmed the beneficial effect of dance on the hippocampus region of the brain. Dance has an anti-aging effect in mental and physical capacity.

The New Year is celebrated according to the Chinese lunar calendar.

The diviner called sanjinso makes his prognosis from Book of Changes or "Yi Jing"(IChing),the oldest of Chinese classical texts which deeply influenced Confucian thinking.

The Book of Changes is a collection of taoist advices,annotated by Confucius,the great scholar, being read as a guide to moral perfection. Confucianism involves a moral disposition the cultivation of virtues.

––––––––––

Yin and Yang energies of the universe work together in perfect harmony. The relationship between humans and nature (Tao) gives rise to the change of things.

The consultation is carried out through the "eight trigrams" (chinese:Bagua) produced by the four forms of Yin and Yang and their permutations.

The trigrams consist of three lines that are either solid (Yang) or divided (Yin).The 64 symbolic hexagrams(two trigrams)are constructed on interaction between the yin and yang energies.

Studies involved in the effect of religion on physical health have revealed it has a positive attribution to lifestyle.

Buddhist monks believe positive emotions can be cultivated.Spirituality seems to strengthen neurons in the left prefrontal cortex by inhibiting stress.

Durkheim saw religion as the institution that gave humanity the strongest sense of collective consciousness.

Basically,religion was a particularly important source of solidarity that enclosed beliefs that most people in society have in common.

Okinawans identify themselves in their culture derived from ancestral belief. The religious community is the largest source of social support outside of the family.

CHAPTER 4

The laws of the nature

Okinawa was once part of the Ryūkyū Kingdom and the cultural relationship with China was destined to be maintained for long time.

Chinese immigrants traveled to Ryūkyūs as cultural envoys from Fujian province during the Ming dynasty.

The descendants were the cultural elite of the Ryūkyū Kingdom.They were also consultants in the Chinese tradition of "Feng Shui"or geomancy,literally translated as"wind and water".

The "way of nature" aims at harmonizing human existence with the laws of nature. The harmony depends on the primordial energies behind the continuous change.

Wind and water are the original elements in nature,interacting constantly to maintain the balance.

These elements represent two different aspects of "Qi"energy:

1.Water (mizu) represents the descending life force

2.Wind (kaze) represents the expanding life force

The most auspicious location take advantage of the harmonic water flow.The water element nourishes the livings in the world, benefiting the nature with Qi life force.

Feng shui uses "Lo Pan compass" to maximize the flow of positive Qi by aligning the site with 8 directions or "Bagua" which represents fluctuations of yin and yang.

The protection from negative influences was the result of a balance of Yang and Yin opposing energies within environment.

In Feng Shui,the dragon and the tiger represent Yin and Yang energies.

The dragon is the celestial guardian of the east compass direction. The dragon controls over water element.

The tiger is the celestial protector of the west compass direction.The tiger represents the force and ensures prosperity of descendants.

Okinawan villages are located in the mountain side to get a balance of yin-yang energy embracing the village.

Fukugi trees (Garcinia subelliptica) were planed around the houses to provide for protection from typhoons and floods.

Additionally, house construction rites are often performed by ritual specialists (Fungshi) in charge to protect the house against misfortune.

Amulets stones called "Ishiganto" are commonly found at forked roads to guard against evil spirits travelling in straight lines.

The royal tombs of the Ryūkyū Kingdom are located at Tamaudun by King Sho Shin. The configuration of the tomb was introduced form China's Fujian province.

The turtle-shaped tomb(kameko-baka) is associated with North direction. In Feng Shui,turtle reflects the fundamental aspect of the protection from unfavorable currents,winds and water.

The scholar Guo Pu wrote "The Book of Burial" that was considered the handbook to ensure the most auspicious site for burials.The tomb is the continuation of life after death.

The Shuri Castle is the most representative of Feng Shui, now a recognized UNESCO World Heritage Site.

The castle is situated on a hill,facing the port of Naha to provide the primordial energy of water to the castle.

The gate of welcome is the Kankaimon, protected by two stone shisa talismans (lion dogs) as guardians against evil fires.

After the II World War,all the past of Shuri Court has been revived with the Buku Buku Tea ceremony.

The Kumemura community served the ritual to entertain accredited delegations from China. The sense of hospitality (omotenashi) is expressed by a deeply effort in welcoming visitors through tea ceremony.

The jasmine tea (Sanpin) is believed to have been exported from Chinese province of Fujian. Bubbles on the top of the green tea can be made only with ocean 's water.

The flavored tea can be directly found from nature,typically made of a blend of green tea and jasmine petals. The antioxidants within both plants can help with the signs of aging.

The way of tea (chao-dao) is strongly rooted in the Chinese idea to feel the nature with peaceful heart for offering calm in the mind.

Tea ceremony was based on the perception of "Wabi-Sabi".

The sensory experience required a quiet space to embody the state of tranquillity and semplicity."Wabi" represents the simplicity or quietness and "Sabi" is the natural imperfection or serenity.

Okinawan culture recognises that human life is a part of nature, so closely influenced by changes in environment. The laws of nature help Okinawans achieve peace and prosperity in the present.

CHAPTER 5

The legend of the white crane

The Ryūkyū Kingdom signed the agreement with China to become a vassal for the purpose of trade and cultural exchange. Fujian province is the area which historically interacted much more with Okinawa.

The chinese community taught in secret the "Bubishi"(Wu Bu Shu),a compilation of 32 essays taken mostly from "White Crane" kenpo combat .It is believed that female taoist created the the "White Crane" style which was introduced to Okinawa from Fujian Province.

The chinese God of art and longevity is found in the Bubishi. Fujian Opera performers trained in White Crane style and martial forms were hidden in the movement of dance.

They had connection with the secret societies (Triad) which helped Chinese immigrants and formed a hidden parallel state within imperial China.

Chinese culture was brought to Ryûkyû by the 36 Min families.The white crane is a mythologic animal related to the idea of immortality.

The secret text contains also herbal Medicine (Die Da Jiu) for herbal treatment.

It is commonly known that chinese masters were expected to know the rudiments of medical herbs and vital points of Agupuncture.

The "Kenpo Gokui"Poems refers to the "gō-jū" combination of softness(Yin) and hardness (Yang) in the White Crane Kenpo.

The formalized sequence (chinese:quan;japanese:kata) were performed very slowly to unify the mind (Yang) with the body (Yin).

Bubishi describes the core of Chinese alchemy to achieve longevity by conserving Jing,Qi,Shen or "three treasures".

Disciples become conscious of their spiritual energy (Shen) of the Heart,through continual transformations of Yin and Yang aspects of internal energy.

The natural breath from the lower abdomen (dantian) promotes the movement of Qi (air)in the body. The coordination of the body with the breath is the balance of the Yin-Yang.

The techniques of control breathing were used to preserve "Jing" life essence which is inherited from birth.

Jing can be restored through herbals, as well as through breathing exercises. Premature aging is the result of the reduction of native Jing due to excessive stress,menstruation and sexual activity.

Okinawans trained body with series of exercises to reinforce all the parts of the body. Since ancient times,"Hojo Undo" is the supplementary training for developing the Qi.

Hojo Undo method uses chinese tools, made from wood and stone:box of sand,bamboo sticks,heavy stone,bar with weights,holding jars,stone padlock.

The internal training use weapons techniques for development of internal energy.The basic instruction of Hojo Undo can be found in the Bubishi.

Okinawans were prohibited from using weapons due to restrictions when the island was made a part of Japan.Okinawans practiced the chinese weapon systems (kobudō)secretly.

The tonfa is the famous side handle baton police in modern times.The nunchaku was chained sticks popularized by Bruce Lee.

The martial styles of Okinawa were generally referred to the area of origin in the island:Shuri-te, Naha-te and Tomari-te.

The breathing naturally is a peculiarity of Shorin-ryu from Shuri-Te and the Shotokan karate.

Gichin Funakoshi was author of the first publication on Bubishi's anthology: "Ryukyu Kenpo Karate-jutsu." He was a member of the Peckin Warrior caste who studied Shuri-te style,the fighting art of Shuri Court.

Master Funakoshi played an important role in the creation of the modern Shotokan Karate-Do with the motto of "no first attack"."

The philosophy of Shotokan Karate-Do are twenty principles(Niju Kun) which stress purification of mind in the practitioner.

Conflict can be transformed into its opposite according to Yin-Yang principles. It was Funakoshi's belief that the Karate-Do preserve "the way of life" based on the three virtues:kindness, simplicity and modesty.

The Karate-Do comes from a system of training in Okinawa that contribute to preserve the quality of of life.

Aging leads to a general decline in body functions that affects quality Remaining active will prevent the   onset   of   age-related   disorders.

CHAPTER 6

The way of life

Traditional Chinese medicine (TCM)was actively incorporated in the Ryūkyū Kingdom when delegations were sent to China and helped introduce the way of life.

The aspects of Yin and Yang are the natural forces that must always be in balance. Traditional Chinese Medicine considers two poles produced by the Qi moviment.

In The Yellow Emperor's Classic of Internal Medicine, it was written:

"Heaven was created by the concentration of Yang, the force of light, earth was created by the concentration of Yin, the forces of darkness....".

Since Yin and Yang are complementary in nature,the activities of the organism maintains a dynamic equilibrium.

The clinical diagnosis determinate Yin and Yang nature of the disease resulting from the influence of the environment:

a)heat symptoms are caused by Yin deficiency

b)cold symptoms are caused by Yang deficiency

Yin embodies the cold energy,whereas Yang is the warm energy.

The interplay of Yin and Yang produce the "Five Phases" of the nature:Wood,Fire,Earth, Metal,Water.

In the Yin-Yang theory,the "Five elements" represents the seasons which keep "Five Organs Network" in harmony:

1.Wood(Spring)corresponds to the Liver
2.Fire(Summer)corresponds to the Heart
3.Earth(Late Summer)corresponds to the Spleen
4.Metal(Autumn)corresponds to the Lung
5.Water(Winter)corresponds to the Kidneys

There are different natural climatic factors which adversely become pathogenic factors:

1.wind affects the Liver
2.heat affects the Heart
3.dampness affects Spleen
4.dryness affects the Lung
5.cold affects the Kidneys

Under these natural natural factors,the body is able to adapt itself to the changes of the climate.

The Five Elements theory asserts that each element creates cycles of generation (sheng) and control(ko)which keeps the body in balance:

1.Wood generates Fire and inhibits Earth
2.Fire generates Earth and restrains Metal
3.Earth supports Metal and controls Water
4.Metal vitalizes Water and inhibits Wood
5.Water nourishes Wood and restrains Fire

The cycles gives an idea of general balance in nature in the same way that a mother nourishes her child.

The Yellow Emperor's Classic of Internal Medicine often speaks of Qi and Blood together as interdependent relationship.

The Meridians are the passages through which blood and Qi nourish Five organs throughout the body.

According to the biological clock,the five organs store up Qi and regulate its moviment.It is important for the body a deep sleep between 11 pm and 5 am to help Qi promotes the circulation of blood.

Chinese Medicine focused on restoring a deficiency of Qi and blood.Therefore,the insufficiency of the healthy Qi should be supplemented with herbs.

The World Health Organization (WHO) estimates that 80 percent of the world population use herbal medicine for primary health care.

WHO also reports that Japan has the highest per capita consumption of herbal medicine in the world. Much of the earliest literature about medical herbs comes from ancient Chinese herbal texts which had been lost in China.

After the Meiji Restoration,the imperial physicians contributed greatly to the revival of the chinese herbal medicine,also known as Kampo medicine. The Ishinpo is the first japanese medical text compiled by Yasuyori Tanba.

After its introduction from China,Kampo became a variant of Chinese traditional medicine,that involves the extensive use of herbs.The term "Kampo" literally means "method from the Han period" from ancient China.

In terms of treatment,the herb specific properties can influence the Yin and Yang of the body. Herbs have been found to have energy levels defined by two characteristics: Yin is reducing, Yang is tonifying.

The Kampo physician observes the tongue and the pulse of the blood.

The diagnosis (sho) indicates specific treatments on improving the circulation of Qi and blood.

The Chinese Five Elements system classifies herbs according to five flavors that mark the two fundamental energies of yin and yang:

1.Spicy(Yang)invigorates Lung

2.Sweet(Yang)invigorates Spleen

3.Bitter(Yin)invigorates Heart

4.Sour(Yin)invigorates Liver

5.Salty(Yin)invigorates Kidneys

————

These herbs use the energy derived from the five elements to ward off pathogenic influences.

In the diagnosis tonifying herbs are the most essential procedure to restoring balance of energy by nourishing the body.

————

The following are some of the common herbs used in kampo medicines:

ginger,scutellaria,kudzu,ginseng,mint,magnolia,longan,liquorice,gentian,gardenia,fennel,loquat,corydalis,shiitake,chrysanthemum,astragalus,mugwort,burdock,angelica,lotus,perilla,rhizome,rehmanni,peonia.

————

Most herbal formulas are widely available as pills, powders and medical liquors.The herbal teas and soups were also recommended by Chinese herbalists to absorbtheir properties.

The Department of Pharmaceutical Affairs of the Ministry of Health and Welfare approved many of the traditional formulas,which are prescribed by Western-trained medical doctors in Japan.

––––––––––

Many drugs have been developed from chinese herbs for the treatments such as for Alzheimer's disease and other forms of dementia affecting millions of elders.

Today,Kampo medicine is well-integrated into japanese health care system,including Okinawa Prefecture.

CHAPTER 7

The harmony of the five senses

The concept that food is medicine (nuchi gusui) flourished as the integral part of folk medicine in Okinawa. The Yellow Emperor's Classic of Internal Medicine was the most important text on food therapy.

Traditional Chinese medicine views the stomach as a the cauldron that turns the food into energy,providing supplements Qi and Blood. The stomach holds the food, while the spleen transports and transforms the food.

The body needs a balance of Yin and Yang in order to be healthy:Yin persons must consume more Yang foods and the opposite for Yang persons.

Foods are classified as having either yin or yang qualities:

1.Yin foods are considered cold and cool in nature such as sake,sugar,oil,spices,vegetables and fruits

2.Yang foods are warm and hot in nature such as poultry,seafood,meat,fish,salt

3.Neutral foods are both Yin and Yang in nature such as beans,seeds,rice,root vegetables, seaweeds

---

It is stated in The Medical Classic of the Yellow Emperor:"Human life originates in the Qi of Heaven and Earth,and develops according to the normal order of the four seasons."

.Foods tends to have all five element energies corresponding to the four seasons.People of Okinawa live in harmony with nature(ishoku dogen)by eating fresh ingredients harvested on the island

The living habits are linked to the four seasons to maintain the unity between the internal and external environment of the human body.

There are typically three daily meals,breakfast,lunch and dinner.

They are based on the the following courses:soup,tofu,fruit,soba,seaweeds,rice,vegetable,tea

.

Human emotions are strongly associated with the function of internal organs,so well-balanced diet will enjoy different foods:

1.green foods balance anger(Liver)

2.red foods balance joy(Heart)

3.yellow foods balance anxiety(Spleen)

4.white foods balance grief(Lungs)

5.dark foods balance fear(Kidneys)

The colors of foods correspond to the Five elements which have have different effects on health.

Clinically,the human emotions are endogenous,they can directly affect the internal organs due to disharmony of Qi and blood.

Ryukyu Court Cuisine has been strongly influenced by the text "Gozen Honzo" from Fujian Province which listed the herbal therapeutic uses.

The idea of food medicine is considered a key element to longevity.The way to create balance in the body is a variety of the five tastes and colors in food preparation.

Each taste nourishes a specific organ correlated with a season:

1.sour(Wood)acts on the Liver in the spring
2.bitter(Fire)acts on the Heart in mid-summer
3.sweet(Earth)acts on the Spleen in the late summer
4.spicy(Metal)acts on the Lungs in the autumn
5.salty(Water)acts on the Kidneys in the winter

In Greek,the term Panacea is usually used to indicate something to completely solve a problem. Japanese mythology reported miso as a gift from the gods for longevity.

The fermentation process produced natural compounds involved in protecting against free radical damage.The fermented soybean paste is made from rice,inocculated with koji fungus.

It is said that Liu An,the grandson of Chinese Emperor Liu Bang,failed but created tofu in his efforts to produce immortal elixir.

Tofu became an essential ingredient in the miso soup since ancient times. The consumption of miso soup is beneficial for preventing the negative effects of unhealthy lifestyle.

The anti-aging property is attributed to its high content of antioxidants,using naturally acquired ingredients.

In Okinawa,miso soups mainly are served for breakfast or dinner to improve digestion and absorption of nutrients.

When ingredients are in balance,life can be sustained. Japanese doctors studied the beneficial combination of five ingredients in miso soup for the treatment of degenerative diseases such as cancer.

The Japan Ministry of Health, Labour and Welfare recommends that one consume 30 different foods daily in order to get a wide variety of nutrients.

———

Okinawan culture is a model of balanced diet which lies in the respect for nature.The goal is to maintain a steady state or equilibrium in the body.

Local foods combined with tranquillity and physical activity are the secrets of their elixir of long life.

CHAPTER 8

The Champuru culture

The term "Champuru" is used to describe the mixed food culture due to its long history of trade .Okinawa was for centuries used as a "gateway" between Japan and China.

Since the Ryūkyū Kingdom had served as a tributary state to China, Okinawan cooks traveled to learn Fujian cuisine (Min Culture)in order to entertain imperial emissaries.

The Ryukyuan palace cuisine incorporates cultural practices and ingredients that meld together into the Okinawan unique taste.

The foods of Fujian province are closely related to Okinawan cuisine.The cuisine is rich in quality nutritious ingredients from the sea and the mountains (yin-Yang).

The Okinawan dishes incorporate some ingredients from Fujian province.For example,the pork is native from China and every part is eaten.The popular "Goya champuru" is an Okinawan dish that represents a mixture of cultural exchange.

Champuru cuisine is also known for the soups,applying a wide variety of herbs harvested on the island to flavorthe food.

The main aspect of the daily diet is that its dishes are served in soup made of pork or vegetables in kombu seaweed broth.

To find out more about the Okinawa diet, the list below is just a starting insight into Okinawan ingredients with anti-aging properties:

Acerola

Nature:Yang

Element:Earth

Taste:Sweet

The acerola(Malpighia glabra)is a cherry like fruit of the genus Prunus that grows in Okinawa.The juice is very popular as dressing for seafood.

Actions:tonifies Spleen,Qi

Nutrients:bioflavonoids,vitamins B-C,potassium

Indications:diarrhea,dysentery

Properties:may prevent the risk of macular degeneration, Alzheimer

———————

Adzuki beans

Nature:Neutral

Element:Earth

Taste:Sweet

The red beans(Vigna angularis),also known as adzuki beans,are the leguminous fruit-pods of belongs to the Fabaceae family. The red-colored beans were believed to ward off bad luck.

Actions:benefits Liver,Qi,Blood

Nutrients:fiber,vitamin B,zinc,copper,magnesium

Indications:diabetes,difficult urination

Properties:may prevent the risk of heart attacks,osteoporosis

Asa seaweed

Nature:Neutral

Element:Water

Taste:Salty

Asa(Ipomoea aquatica)is a green seaweed,known as sea lettuce,harvested around Ojima-island during the low tide.It is usually used for soup in China.

Actions:tonifies Kidneys,Qi

Nutrients:vitamin B,iron

Indications:abdominal pain,cough

Properties:may prevent the risk of of heart diseases,cancer

Asparagus

Nature:Yin

Element:Fire

Taste:Bitter

Asparagus is considered part of the Asparagaceae family.Asparagus roots are an important folk medicine listed as a top-grade in the Chinese Herbalism.

Actions:tonifies Lungs,Blood

Nutrients:fiber B,vitamins K-C

Indications:hypertension,high cholesterol

Properties:may prevent the risk of cancer,heart diseases

Bamboo shoots

Nature:Yin

Element:Earth

Taste:Sweet

The bamboo plant(Pleioblastus linearis) is evergreen perennial plant of the grass family which grows naturally on the Island of Okinawa.Shoots are culms of the bamboo plant,seasonal ingredient particularly in China.

Actions:tonifies Spleen,Qi

Nutrients:fiber,vitamin B,iron,potassium

Indications:diarrhea,dysentery

Properties:may prevent the risk of heart diseases,cancer

Banana

Nature:Yin

Element:Earth

Taste:Sweet

Shima banana(Musa acuminata colla) belongs to the family of Musaceae.It is one of the widely cultivated crops in the tropical and subtropical zones.

Actions:tonify Lungs,Blood

Nutrients:antioxidants lutein,beta-carotenes,vitamins

A-C,phosphorus,magnesium,calcium,potassium

Indications:constipation,cough

Properties:may prevent the risk of macular degeneration, osteoporosis

Bean sprouts
Nature:Yin
Element:Earth
Taste:Sweet
Bean sprouts have been prized since ancient times, not only in Japan but also in China,also known as Moyashi.
Bean sprouts are rich in nutrition.
Nutrients:fiber,vitamins A-B-C,asparagines,potassium
Actions:tonifies Spleen,Blood
Indications:anemia,constipation
Properties:may prevent the risk of diabetes,cancer

———————

Bitter melon
Nature:Yin
Element:Fire
Taste:Bitter
Bitter melon(Momordica charantia) or bitter gourd belongs to the Cucurbitaceae family,referred as Goya in Okinawa.
The green plant is used as an effective blood purifier in China.
Nutrients:vitamins A-C,iron
Actions:tonifies Lungs,Blood
Indications:constipation,anti-inflammatory
Properties:may prevent the risk of heart diseases, diabetes

Burdock

Nature:Yin

Element:Fire

Taste:Bitter

Okinawan burdock ,also known as gobo root, is a vegetable that belongs to the family of Asteraceae. The folk medicine used burdock as a remedy to improve digestion.

Actions:tonifies Heart,Qi,Blood

Nutrients:fiber,vitamins B-C-E,manganese,magnesium

Indications:sore throat,comon cold

Properties:may prevent the risk of cancer,diabetes

———————

Cabbage

Nature:Yin

Element:Fire

Taste:Bitter

The napa cabbage(Brassica campestris)is a leafy vegetable of Brassica family known as Hakusai,symbol of prosperity.

Chinese Medicine recommends eating cabbage as it greatly clear toxins.

Actions:tonifies Kidneys,Qi

Nutrients:fiber,carotene-ß,lutein,vitamins C-K ,calcium

Indications:constipation,difficulty urinating

Properties:may prevent the risk of Alzheimer,macular degeneration

Canola
Nature:Yin
Element:Wood
Taste:Sour
Canola oil is a vegetable oil derived from pressing rape seeds of the Brassicaceae family.Canola oil is a type of cooking oil that most commonly used in China.
Actions:tonifies Spleen,Qi
Nutrients:vitamins E-K,omega-3 -6 fatty acids
Indications:cough,dysentery
Properties:may prevent the risk of Alzheimer,diabetes

Carrot
Nature:Neutral
Element:Metal
Taste:Spicy
Carrot is a root vegetable in genus,Allium,known asShimaninjin.Okinawa Island is widely covered in carrot fields.The majority of carrots are included in salads and soups.
Actions:tonifies Lungs,Blood
Nutrients:vitamins A-B-C-K,potassium
Indications:indigestion,eye weakness
Properties:may prevent the risk of macular degeneration,heart diseases

Chrysanthemum

Nature:Neutral
Element:Fire
Taste:Bitter
The Chrysanthemum(Chrysanthemum indicum) is cultivated all over the Okinawa island.
Chrysanthemum tea is a flower-based infusion beverage made from chrysanthemum flowers which are most popular in China.
Actions:tonifies Lungs,Blood
Nutrients:vitamins A-C
Indications:high pressure,anti-inflammatory
Properties:may prevent the risk of heart diseases,cancers

————

Chicken

Nature:Yang
Element:Earth
Taste:Sweet
Chicken is very popular meat with high amount of protein and low fat content.Chicken is used for blood deficiency in the soups.
The chicken contains anti-inflammatory substances which control inflammatory white blood cells.
Actions:tonifies Liver,Qi,Blood
Nutrients:vitamin B,potassium,iron,zinc
Indications:weakness,bronchitis
Properties:may prevent the risk of heart diseases, macular degeneration

Cucumber

Nature:Cold
Element:Fire
Taste:Bitter
Cucumber(Cucumis sativus)belongs to the Cucurbitaceae family in the gourd family,called nabera in Okinawa.
The cucumber is commonly eaten in stir-fries and soups.
Actions:tonifies Lungs,Qi,Blood,
Nutrients:fiber,vitamins
A-C,calcium,magnesium,phosphorus
Indications:diarrhea, sore throat
Properties:may prevent the risk of diabetes,heart diseases

Daikon

Nature:Yin
Element:Wood
Taste:Sour
Daikon(Raphanus sativus) is the white radish known as Chinese radish.White radishes can help with food stagnation and the nutrient properties of leaves serve as antioxidants.
Actions:tonifies Liver,Qi,Blood
Nutrients:beta-carotene,vitamins A-B-C,calcium
Indications:dry cough,bronchitis
Properties:may prevent the risk of osteoporosis,cancer

Dragon fruit

Nature:Yin

Element:Earth

Taste:Sweet

The Dragon plant is a vine of the genus Hylocereus,also known as pitaya.The skin is red-skinned with red flesh.

The flowers are ornate with fragrant scent.

Actions:tonifies Liver,Qi,Blood

Nutrients:antioxidants,vitamins B-C

Indications:bacteria and fungi,antibacterial

Properties:may prevent the risk of diabetes,cancer

Edamame
Nature:Yin
Element:Earth
Taste:Sweet
Edamame is a dicotyledonous plant,belonging to the family of Leguminosae in the genus Glycine.
Pods are boiled in salted water and served in a bowl as a snack.
Actions:tonifies Liver,Qi,Blood
Nutrients:fiber,vitamins B-C-K, potassium,calcium
Indications:high pressure,high cholesterol
Properties:may prevent the risk of heart diseases,osteoporosis

Eggplant
Nature:Neutral
Element:Earth
Taste:Sweet
Eggplant(Solanum melongena)or aubergine is a member of the genus Solanum.
The seasonal vegetable helps to improve food stagnation.
Actions:tonifies Spleen,Qi
Nutrients:vitamins B-C-K,magnesium,phosphorus,copper
Indications:dysentery,diarrhea
Properties:may prevent the risk of cancer,osteoporosis

————

Fennel
Nature:Yang
Element:Wood
Taste:Sour
The fennel(Foeniculum vulgare)is called ichoba in Okinawa.
The perennial plant is a member of the Apiaceae.
The seeds are commonly used in the prevention of premature aging in China.
Actions:tonifies Kidneys,Qi
Nutrients:fiber,vitamins
A-C,calcium,potassium,phosphorus
Indications:stomachache,colic
Properties:may prevent the risk of osteoporosis,cancer

Fish

Nature: Neutral
Element:Water
Taste:Salty
Okinawa offers plenty of tropical fish but Okinawans eat relatively little seafood.
Zamami village became a center of katsuobushi,a dried bonito fillet essential to Japanese cuisine.
Actions:tonifies Kidneys,Qi
Nutrients:vitamins B-D,coenzyme Q10,omega-3
Indications:low energy,arteriosclerosis
Properties:may prevent the risk of heart diseases,Alzheimer

———————

Garlic

Nature:Yang
Element:Fire
Taste:Bitter
Garlic (Allium sativum) or "Nira" belongs to the family of Alliaceae.
The herb plant have traditionally been used for maintenance of health and treatment of diseases.
Actions:tonifies Qi,Blood
Nutrients:allicin,βcarotene,vitamin C,potassium,zinc
Indications:high cholesterol,infections
Properties:may prevent the risk of heart diseases,cancer

Ginger

Nature:Yang

Element:Fire

Taste:Bitter

Gettou is a member of the ginger family cultivated in all over Okinawa.

Ginger root can be used as a spice.It is effective as a cure for regulating intestinal functions.

Actions:tonifies Lungs,Blood

Nutrients:fiber,vitamin B,polyphenol,potassium,calcium,

Indications:cold,arthritis

Properties:may prevent the risk of heart disease,osteoporosis

———————

Goat

Nature: Yang

Element:Earth

Taste:Sweet

The custom of eating goat meat came to Okinawa from China about 600 years ago.

Okinawan people consume dairy foods such as goat milk and cheese.

Actions:tonifies Qi,Blood

Nutrients:linoleic acid,vitamin B,calcium

Indications:insomnia,fatigue

Properties:may prevent the risk of osteoporosis,heart diseases

Green Onion
Nature:Yang
Element:Metal
Taste:Spicy
Green onions(scallions)are also known as the Chinese onions of the genus Allium.
In Chinese medicine green onions are a key ingredient in a cold-fighting soup.
Actions:tonifies Lungs,Blood
Nutrients:quercetin,vitamins B-C,K,magnesium
Indications:congestion,arthritis
Properties:may prevent the risk of heart diseases,cancer

————————

Green pepper
Nature:Neutral
Element:Earth
Taste:Sweet
Shishito is a small green pepper(Piman)from the Piperaceae family,the genus Zanthoxylum.
It is also used for treatment in Traditional Chinese Medicine.
Actions:tonifies Spleen,Qi
Nutrients:fiber,vitamins A-C-E
Indications:osteoarthritis,rheumatoid arthritis
Properties:may prevent the risk of osteoporosis,heart diseases

Guava
Nature:Yang
Element:Earth
Taste:Sweet
Guava(Psidium guajava)is tropical fruit in the Myrtle family of the genus Psidium.
The phytotherapic plant have been used in traditional medicine to treat malaria.
Actions:tonifies Spleen,Qi
Nutrients:fiber,lycopene,vitamins A-C,potassium,calcium,
omega 3-6 fatty acids
Indications:constipation,dysentery
Properties:may prevent the risk of diabetes,maculardegeneration

———————

Hibiscus
Nature:Yin
Element:Earth
Taste:Sweet
Hibiscus(Pedanius Dioscorides)is a versatile plant,genus of flowering plants in the family Malvaceae,otherwise known as the akabana.
The tea made from hibiscus flowers is known for its red color.
Actions:tonifies Liver,Qi,Blood
Nutrients:anthocyanins,vitamin C
Indications:high pressure,bad cholesterol
Properties:may prevent the risk of heart diseases,diabetes

Hijiki

Nature:Yang

Element:Water

Taste:Salty

Hijiki(Sargassum fusiforme)is a green seaweed, harvested in Okinawa for centuries.

It aids in stimulating the release of digestive enzymes,supporting the absorption of nutrients.

Actions:tonifies Kidneys,Qi

Nutrients:fiber,vitamin K,calcium,iron,iodine

Indications:stomach bacteria,anti-viral

Properties:may prevents the risk of osteoporosis,heart diseases

---

Jasmine

Nature:Yang

Element:Earth

Taste:Sweet

Jasmine is commonly used base flavor for the "Sanpin-cha" or jasmine Green tea.

Jasmine is a tonic herb used in Chinese medicine for loss of appetite and weight loss by speeding up metabolism.

Actions:tonifies Heart,Qi,Blood

Nutrients:catechins,vitamins A-B

Indications:stress,chronic inflammation

Properties:may prevent the risk of diabetes,heart diseases

Konjac
Nature:Yin
Element:Earth
Taste:Sweet
Konjac is a perennial plant of the genus Amorphophallus, also known primarily for its tuber-like form.
The use of konjac has a long culinary history in China and Japan.
Actions:tonifies Kidneys,Qi,Blood
Nutrients:fiber,glucomannan
Indications:artherosclerosis,high cholesterol
Properties:may prevents the risk of diabetes,heart diseases

Kombu

Nature:Yin

Element:Water

Taste:Salty

Kombu(Laminaria japonica)is the most consumed seaweed of
Phaeophyceae family.

During the Ryukyu Kingdom period,Kombu was one of China's major exports,so it was introduced into Okinawa.

Actions:tonifies Kidneys,Qi,Blood

Nutrients:fiber,iodine,vitamin K

Indications:cough,mucus

Properties:may prevents the risk of macular degeneration,cancer

Kudzu
Nature:Yin
Element:Wood
Taste:Sour
Kudzu(pueraria lobata)is perennial vine native to the tropical areas of Japan and China.
The medicinal root is often used it for cooking soup in southern China.
Action:tonifies Liver,Qi,Blood
Nutrients:vitamins A-D
Indications:diarrhea,headache
Properties:may prevent the risk of osteoporosis,heart diseases

———

Kumquats
Nature:Yang
Element:Earth
Taste:Sweet
Kumquats Citrus japonica) are the fruits of a small tree in the Rutaceae family,also known as kinkan.
They are smaller in size than most orange varieties.They have been grown and cultivated for thousands of years in China.
Action:tonifies Liver,Blood
Nutrients:fiber,beta-carotene,vitamins A-C,calcium
Indications:sore throats,diabetes
Properties:may prevent the risk of osteoporosis,macular degeneration

Lemon
Nature:Yin
Element:Wood
Taste:Sour
Lemon(Citrus depressa)is an unripe fruit,flowering plant family Rutaceae that is grown in Okinawa,called shikuwasa which means sour food.
Actions:tonifies Liver,Qi,Blood
Nutrients:lutein,vitamins A-B-C,calcium,potassium
Indications:sore throat,rheumatism
Properties:may prevent the risk of cancer,diabetes

Longan
Nature:Yin
Element:Earth
Taste:Sweet
The longan(Dimocarpus Longan)is one of tropical members of the berry family.The longan means "dragon eye"in Chinese.
The fruit's health benefits include anti-aging properties.
Actions:tonifies Heart,Qi,Blood
Nutrients:vitamins B-C,phosphorus
Indications:anxiety,insomnia
Properties:may prevent the risk of Alzheimer,heart diseases

Lotus
Nature:Neutral
Element:Earth
Taste:Sweet
Lotus (Nelumbo nucifera)is a herbaceous perennial of the Nelumbonaceae family,also known as renkon.
Lotus seeds are sweet and astringent,used for loss of appetite and weight loss.
Actions:tonifies Spleen,Qi
Nutrients:fiber,vitamins A-B-C,potassium,magnesium
Indications:gastritis,colitis
Properties:may prevent the risk of macular degeneration, heart diseases

----

Mango
Nature:Yin
Element:Earth
Taste:Sweet
Mango is the tropical fruit belonging to the flowering plant genus Mangifera,introduced from Taiwan.
According to chinese medicine,mango is the best fruit for health
benefits.
Actions:tonifies Spleen,Qi
Nutrients:vitamins A-B,potassium
Indications:cough,nausea
Properties:may prevent the risk of diabetes,heart diseases

Mitsuba
Nature:Yang
Element:Fire
Taste:Bitter
Mitsuba(Cryptotaenia japonica)is a member of the Apiaceae family, also known as Japanese parsley. It can be used as a seasoning or potency tonic.
Actions:tonifies Kidneys,Qi
Nutrients:vitamins A-B-C-E-K,calcium,iron,potassium,zinc
Indications:indigestion,stomachache
Properties:may prevent the risk of cancer,osteoporosis

Mozuku

Nature:Yang

Element:Water

Taste:Salty

Mozuku(Cladosiphon okamuranus)is a popular seaweed,that is grown in Okinawa.
Mozuku is preserved with salt through the rest of the year.

Actions:tonifies Kidneys,Qi

Nutrients:fiber fucoidan

Indications:cough,mucus

Properties:may prevent the risk of cancer,diabetes

Mugwort

Nature:Yang

Element:Fire

Taste:Bitter

Mugwort(Artemisia Vulgaris)is an aromatic plant in the genus Artemisia,often called fuchiba. Mugwort leaves are consumed in the spring.

The medicinal usage of mugwort date back for thousands of years.

Actions:tonifies Spleen,Qi

Nutrients:flavonoids,calcium,potassium

Indications:anxiety,menstrual pain

Properties:may prevent the risk of cancer,osteoporosis

Mustard
Nature:Yang
Element:Wood
Taste:Sour
Mizuna(Brassica juncea)or japanese mustard is a close cultivar type in Brassica rapa group.
Karashi mustard is made from the crushed seeds of Brassica juncea and sold in paste form.
Actions:tonifies Lungs,Blood
Nutrients:fiber,vitamins B-C-K,iron,calcium,magnesium
Indications:difficulty urinating,cough
Properties:may prevent the risk of Alzheimer,osteoporosis

Octopus

Nature:Neutral
Element:Water
Taste:Sweet
Octopus vulgaris(tako)is a cephalopod,low in calories but is high in saturated fat.
The seafood is a great source of omega 3,ideal to stimulate the brain growth.
Actions:tonifies Kidneys,Qi
Nutrients:vitamin B,cacium,selenium,omega 3 fats
Indications:anxiety,hypertension
Properties:may prevent the risk of Alzheimer,heart diseases

————

Okra

Nature:Neutral
Element:Earth
Taste:sweet
The okra plant (Hibiscus esculentus) is a perennial flowering plant in the Malvaceae family.
Okra bears green colored pods,also known as gumbo.
Actions:tonifies Kidneys,Qi
Nutrients:vitamins B-C
Indications:atherosclerosis,constipation
Properties:may prevent the risk of cancer,heart diseases

Orange

Nature:Yin
Element:Wood
Taste:Sour
Oranges are the hybrid citrus fruit,also known astancan,which belongs to the family Rutaceae.
The chinese fruit is a cross between the pomelo and mandarin fruit.
Actions:tonifies Liver,Qi,Blood
Nutrients:fiber,vitamins B-C,potassium
Indications:cough,hernia
Properties:may prevent the risk of diabetes,macular degeneration

_____

Oysters

Nature:Neutral
Element:Water
Taste:Salty
Pacific Oysters are bivalve mollusks bearing the scientific family name of Ostreidae.
They are often referred to as "sea milk" due to their high nutritional values.
Actions:tonifies Kidneys,Qi,Blood
Nutrients:vitamins B-D,zinc,calcium
Indications:high cholesterol,high pressure
Properties:may prevent the risk of osteoporosis,heart diseases

_____

Papaya

Nature:Neutral
Element:Earth
Taste:Sweet
Papaya is one the most popular fruit in Okinawa which belongs to Caricaceae family.The enzyme papain aids in the digestion of proteins.
Papaya seeds have been used for regulating vital functions.
Actions:tonifies Spleen,Qi
Nutrients:papain,vitamins
A-B,magnesium,calcium,potassium
Indications:constipation,stomachache
Properties:may prevent the risk of osteoporosis,macular degeneration

_____

Passion fruit

Nature:Yin
Element:Fire
Taste:Bitter
Passion fruit(Passiflora edulis)is a dark purple color fruit belonging to the family of Passifloraceae.It looks somewhat like a grapefruit.
The passion fruit has been used to strenghten immunity system since ancient times.
Actions:tonifies Spleen,Qi
Nutrients:fiber,vitamins A-C,potassium,iron
Indications:bad colesterol,insomnia

Properties:may prevents the risk of cancer,osteoporosis

Peanuts

Nature:Neutral

Element:Earth

Taste:Sweet

Peanut(genus Arachis) is a small underground fruit pods of a plant belonging to the Fabaceae family.
In Okinawa peanut is often with Okinawan tofu after being shredded.

Actions:tonifies Spleen,Blood

Nutrients:p-coumaric,vitamin E,calcium,posphorus

Indications:insomnia,hypertension

Properties:may prevents the risk of osteoporosis,Alzheimer

————

Pear

Nature:Yin

Element:Earth

Taste:Sweet

Nashi pear is a several tree of genus Pyrus in the family Rosaceae.
Pears are classified based on their place of origin as Asian pears.This fruit is a symbol of spring.

Actions:tonifies Lungs,Qi

Nutrients:fiber,lutein,vitamins C-K,magnesium

Indications:excess mucus,bronchtis

Properties:may prevent the risk of diabetes,osteoporosis

Perilla
Nature:Neutral
Element:Wood
Taste:Sour
Perilla is a popular spice of the mint family, also kwown as shiso.
Leaves,seeds and stems are used in traditional medicine for nearly 2,000 years.
Actions:tonifies Kidneys,Qi
Nutrients: vitamins A-B, Omega 3-6-9
Indications:intestinal discomforts,seasonal allergies
Properties:may prevent the risk of osteoporosis,heart diseases

---

Pineapple
Nature:Yin
Element:Earth
Taste:Sweet
Pineapple(Ananas)belongs to the Bromeliaceae family.Okinawa is a suitable place to grow pineapples.
Freshlypineapple juice help fend off bone degradation.
Action:tonifies Liver,Qi,Blood
Nutrients:bromelain,vitamin C,magnesum,calcium
Indications:bronchitis,diarrhea
Properties:may prevent the risk of osteoporosis,cancer

Potato
Nature:Neutral
Element:Earth
Taste:Sweet
Sweet potatoes (Ipomoea batatas)are tuberous crops belonging to the family of Convolvulaceae.
The purplecolor tuberous is native from China and rescued villages from famine during typhoons.
Actions:tonifies Spleen,Qi
Nutrients:fiber,beta-carotene,vitamin C,iron,calcium,
magnesium
Indications:ulcer pain,constipation
Properties:may prevent the risk of diabetes,cancer

Pork

Nature:Neutral

Element:Earth

Taste:Sweet

The pork become an indispensable ingredient for Okinawan cuisine.Pigs were introduced to Okinawa by Chinese immigrants.

All parts are eaten in the traditional dishes,thus removing much of the fat.

Actions:tonifies Spleen,Qi

Nutrients:collagen,vitamin B,selenium

Indications:constipation,weakness

Properties:may prevent the risk of cancer,heart diseases

Pumpkin

Nature:Neutral

Element:Earth

Taste:Sweet

Pumpkin (Cucurbita Argyrosperma)is a specie of squash plant of other Cucurbitaceae family.
Pumpkin seeds are being used in chinese medicinal preparations.

Actions:tonifies Spleen,Qi

Nutrients:lycopene,carotene,vitamin A,copper potassium

Indications:dysentery,stomachache

Properties:prevent the risk of macular degeneration,Alzheimer

_____

Rice

Nature:Yang

Element:Earth

Taste:Sweet

The traditional Okinawa diet consists of smaller quantities of rice.
Indica rice is a type called long rice,also known as Japonica rice.

Actions:tonifies Spleen,Qi

Nutrients:fiber,vitamin B

Indications:diarrhea,gastritis

Properties:may prevent the risk of cancer,heart diseases

Sesame seeds

Nature:Neutral

Element:Wood

Taste:Sour

Sesame seeds(Sesamum indicum)are derived from a plant of the Sesamum genus.

Seeds have been used for more than 2,000 years in China for a variety of medical purposes.

Actions:tonifies Liver,Qi,Blood

Nutrients:fiber,vitamin B,magnesium,manganese

Indications:arthritis,constipation

Properties:may prevent the risk of diabetes,cancers

———

Shallot

Nature:Yang

Element:Fire

Taste:Bitter

Shallot is a type of scallions called "shima rakkyo" of the species Allium cepa.

Similar to its relatives,garlic and onion,shallot is the appetizer for awamori sake.

Actions:tonifies Lungs,Blood

Nutrients:allicin,allium,vitamins

A-B-C,potassium,calcium

Indications:common cold,difficulty urinating

Properties:may prevent the risk of diabetes,heart diseases

Shiitake

Nature:Neutral

Element:Earth

Taste:Sweet

Shiitake mushroom(Lentinula edodes)is a medicinal mushroom, used extensively in ancient Chinese medicine.

The black fungus is the staple ingredient in the soups.

Actions:tonifies Lungs,Blood

Nutrients:vitamins A-B-D,potassium,copper,selenium

Indications:anemia,hypertension

Properties:may prevent the risk of cancer,osteoporosis

Spinach
Nature:Neutral
Element:Earth
Taste:Sweet
Handama(Gyunura Crepidioides)is the bicolour colored spinach with purple leaves on one side.
The vegetable grows in subtropical climate and planted as ornamental plant.
Actions:tonifies Spleen,Qi
Nutrients:Vitamins A-K,iron,magnesium,calcium
Indications:constipation,headache
Properties:may prevent the risk of Alzheimer,osteoporosis

Taro

Nature:Neutral

Element:Wood

Taste:Sour

Taro(Colocasia esculenta)is the most widely cultivated species in the Araceae family,also known as Taanmu in Okinawa.

This plant is considered a symbol of fertility in China.

Actions:tonifies Spleen,Qi

Nutrients:fiber,vitamins A-B-C-E,potassium

Indications:arthritis,tendonitis

Properties:may prevent the risk of cancer,heart diseases

Tofu

Nature:Yin

Element:Earth

Taste:Sweet

Tofu(Shima doufu) is product of soybeans, species of legume which have become important for the age-related benefits.

The food of Chinese origin enriched miso soups.

Actions:benefits Spleen,Qi

Nutrients:isoflavones,vitamins B-C-D,calcium,magnesium

Indications:anemia,dysentery

Properties:may prevent the risk of heart diseases,osteoporosis

Tomato
Nature:Yin
Element:Wood
Taste:Sour
The scientific name of tomatoes is Solanum lycopersicum.
China is now one of the world's largest producers of processed tomato products.
Actions:benefits
Nutrients:lycopene,vitamins A-B-C-K,potassium, magnesium
Indications:indigestion,hypertension
Properties:may prevent the risk of cancer,heart diseases

Turmeric
Nature:Yang
Element:Wood
Taste:Sour
Turmeric(Curcuma longa)is a perennial herb of the ginger
family,commonly known as ukonin.
Turmeric herb is cultivated in Fujian where is widely used for a lot of diseases.
Actions:benefits Liver,Qi,Blood
Nutrients:curcumin,vitamins B-C,calcium, magnesium,iron
Indications:anti-Inflammatory,arthritis
Properties:may prevent the risk of cancer,heart diseases

Ume
Nature:Neutral
Element:Wood
Taste:Sour
Ume(Prunus mume)is a species of fruit-bearing tree in the genus Prunus.
Umeboshi are salt plums that has been dried and salt-pickled.
Actions:benefits Liver,Blood
Nutrients:fiber,vitamins A-C,iron
Indications:dysentery, intestinal disorders
Properties:may prevent the risk of cancer,heart diseases

Winter melon

Nature:Yang

Element:Earth

Taste:Sweet

Winter melon (Benincasa hispida) or wax gourd is related to the family of Cucurbitaceae, also known as "Tougan".

Originally cultivated in China,the vine plant is harvested in summer.

Actions:benefits Kidneys,Qi

Nutrients:fiber,vitamins B-C,zinc,iron

Indications:difficulty urinating,high fever

Properties:may prevent the risk of macular degeneration,heart diseases

CONCLUSION

Well-being in older age

Healthy Ageing is defined by World Health Organization (WHO) as the process of developing and maintaining the functional ability that enables well-being in older age.

In 2016,the World Health Assembly developed a comprehensive Global strategy towards a world in which everyone can live a long and healthy life:

1.promoting social participation in community life

2.promoting flexible retirement to remain at work longer

3.promoting a meaningful life,having goals and objectives

4.promoting physical activity for health maintenance

As older adults live longer,they need to be aware of their needs and improve their quality of life.

Maslow proposed to satisfy the instinctual need of a human to reach a "peak experience" in which olders become aware of their own fullest potential.

The psychologist Abraham Maslow developed a theory that suggests a the hierarchy of five basic needs which contribute to gaining longevity:

1.the basic issues of to survival in the daily life

2.the sense of security in order to maintain independence

3.the connection to the community,family and friends

4.the positive self-image and recognition issues

5.the self-actualization,being appreciated for own experience

---

Japan focused investment in public health programs and promote healthy lifestyle habits.

Japanese policies encouraged the institution of "sansedai kazoku" or "three-generation households",where families cares for both children and older adults.

Japan's Senior Citizens Day was designated as national holiday in 1966 with the aim of celebrating the respect for the elderly.

Each Prefectural government sends congratulatory letters and gives awards to elders.

Radio taiso or "radio calisthenics" became thea way of to encourage longevity.

The national exercise play an important role in Japan since the commemoration of the coronation of Emperor Hirohito.

Micronutrient deficiencies are often due to the lack of variety in the foods they eat.Dietary changes seem to have an great impact in older people.

National authorities in the world use World Health Organization guidelines to address the nutritional needs of their elderly populations.

The Japanese government promoted a guidance for dietary intake to educate families on food awareness,including physical activity for the aged.

The Japanese Food Guide which comprises grain dishes,vegetable dishes,fish and meat dishes,and fruits.

Japan joins Expo Milano 2015 with the aim of proposing n heritage of humanity.

The inclusion of the Japanese culinary culture on the list UNESCO's intangible cultural heritage will encourage to contributing to healthy ageing.

The evidence suggests that the development of global strategies will lead to the extension of healthy life in older populations.

APPENDIX
Dashi broth

The vegetarian broth was introduced to Japan from China to live in harmony with nature.

The Buddhist monks used the "rule of five elements which are drawn out naturally from the natural ingredients.Cooking became an extension of meditation practice.

A dashi broth seeks harmony with nature in the chosen ingredients,based on the harmony between the tastes.Seasonal vegetables are believed to provide nutritional balance to the body,mind, and spirit

---

The process of making vegetarian dashi is simple:
1.Cut daikon into bite-sized pieces(Wood)
2.Soak Shitake mushrooms(Earth)in boiling water,slice into bite-sized pieces
3.Boil dried Kombu seaweed(Water)in a large pot
4.Add shiitake mushrooms,chopped ginger(Fire)and green onion(Metal)
6.Drain the soup carefully into a drainer.
If the dashi stock is not used straight away,it will keep in fridge for a week.

Miso soups

The miso soup is a tonic type of food that represents the idea of food medicine.

Recipes can be modified withthe addition of different ingredients,ready at any local supermarket:

1 whole vegetable or potato
5 shiitake mushroom
1 piece Kombu seaweed
1 burdock root
1 daikon root
1 lotus root
1 fennel root
1 bunch chrysanthemum
1 piece fresh ginger
1 green onion
1 shallot
1 green pepper
1 sliced garlic
1 pack bean sprouts
1 large tomato
1 bunch parsley
1 dried longan fruit
1 pack konyac
1 pack mugwort leaves
1 pack peanuts
3 tbsp white miso
2 tbs ground sesame seeds
1 teaspoon ground turmeric
cups of read beans
tofu chunks
1/2 boneless chicken,chopped

_____

Asparagus

_____

Method 1

1.Slice asparagus(Fire)into round slices
2.Peel and cut potatoes(Earth)into half round slices
3.Peel and slice large tomato(Wood)
4.Add mix vegetables to hot dashi into a pot and simmer
5.Add tablespoons of miso(Water)
6.Garnish with chopped green onion(Metal)
Serve immediately

Method 2

1.Slice asparagus(Fire)into round slices

2.Cut block of tofu(Earth)into cubes

3.Peel and cut the carrot(Metal)into thin slices

4.Add mix vegetables to hot dashi into a pot and simmer

5.Add tablespoons of miso(Water)and a block of cubed tofu

6.Garnish with sesame seeds(Wood)

Serve immediately

Bamboo shoots

_____

Method 1

_____

1.Peel and cut bamboo shoots(Earth)julienned
   2.Cut fennel root(Wood)into bite-sized pieces
   3.Peel and cut the carrot(Metal)into thin slices
   4.Add mix vegetables to hot dashi into a pot and simmer
   5.Add tablespoons of miso(Water)
   6.Garnish with parsley(Fire)
   Serve immediately

Method 2

—————

1.Peel and cut bamboo shoots(Earth)julienned
    2.Peel and slice the burdock root(Fire) into pieces
    3.Peel and cut the carrot(Metal)into thin slices
    4.Add mix vegetables to hot dashi into a pot and simmer
    5.Add tablespoons of miso(Water)
    6.Garnish with sesame seeds(Wood)
    Serve immediately

Bean sprouts

_____

Method 1

_____

1. Wash bean sprouts(Earth)in warm water
    2. Cut daikon(Wood)into bite-sized pieces
    3. Peel and slice the burdock root(Fire)into pieces
    4. Add mix vegetables to hot dashi into a pot and simmer
    5. Add tablespoons of miso(Water)
    6. Garnish with chopped green onions(Metal)
Serve immediately

_____

Method 2

_____

1. Wash bean sprouts(Earth)in warm water
    2. Peel and finely slice the garlic(Fire)
    3. Peel and slice large tomato(Wood)
    4. Add mix vegetables to hot dashi into a pot and simmer
    5. Add tablespoons of miso(Water)
    6. Garnish with chopped green onions(Metal)
Serve immediately

Bitter gourd

———————

Method 1

———————

1.Slice seeded bitter gourd(Metal)
  2.Soak shiitake mushrooms(Earth)in warm water,slice into
  bite-sized pieces
  3.Peel and finely slice the garlic(Fire)
  4.Add mix vegetables to hot dashi into a pot and simmer
  5.Add tablespoons of miso(Water)
  6.Garnish with sesame seeds(Wood)
  Serve immediately

———————

Method 2

———————

1.Slice seeded bitter gourd(Metal)
  2.Cut block of tofu into cubes(Earth)
  3.Cut daikon(Wood)into bite-sized pieces
  4.Add mix vegetables to hot dashi into a pot and simmer
  5.Add tablespoons of miso(Water)and a block of cubed
  tofu
  6.Garnish with parsley(Fire)
  Serve immediately

Burdock

Method 1

1.Peel and slice the burdock root(Fire)into pieces
   2.Soak shiitake mushrooms(Earth)in warm water,slice into
   bite-sized pieces
   3.Peel and cut the carrot(Metal)into thin slices
   4.Add mix vegetables to hot dashi into a pot and simmer
   5.Add tablespoons of miso(Water)
   6.Garnish with sesame seeds(Wood)
   Serve immediately

Method 2

1.Peel and slice the burdock root(Fire)into pieces
   2.Peel and cut potatoes(Earth)into half round slices
   3.Peel and slice large tomato(Wood)
   4.Add mix vegetables to hot dashi into a pot and simmer
   5.Add tablespoons of miso(Water)
   6.Garnish with chopped green onions(Metal)
   Serve immediately

Cabbage

_____

Method 1

_____

1.Cut the cabbage into strips(Fire)
    2.Peel and cut potatoes(Earth)into half round slices
    3.Cut daikon(Wood)into bite-sized pieces
    4.Add mix vegetables to hot dashi into a pot and simmer
    5.Add tablespoons of miso(Water)
    6.Garnish with chopped green onions(Metal)
    Serve immediately

_____

Method 2

_____

1.Cut the cabbage into strips(Fire)
    2.Soak shiitake mushrooms(Earth)in warm water, slice
    into bite-sized pieces
    3.Peel the carrots(Metal)and cut into strips
    4.Add mix vegetables to hot dashi into a pot and simmer
    5.Add tablespoons of miso(Water)
    6.Garnish with sesame seeds(Wood)
    Serve immediately

Carrot

_____

Method 1

_____

1.Peel the carrots(Metal)and cut into strips
   2.Peel and cut bamboo shoots(Earth)julienned
   3.Cut fennel root(Wood)into bite-sized pieces
   4.Add mix vegetables to hot dashi into a pot and simmer
   5.Add tablespoons of miso(Water)
   6.Garnish with parsley(Fire)
   Serve immediately

_____

Method 2

_____

1.Peel the carrots(Metal)and cut into strips
   2.Peel and finely slice the garlic(Fire)
   3.Cut the spinach(Earth)into pieces
   4.Add mix vegetables to hot dashi into a pot and simmer
   5.Add tablespoons of miso(Water)
   6.Garnish with sesame seeds(Wood)
   Serve immediately

Chicken

_____

Method 1

_____

1.Peel and cut the carrot(Metal)into thin slices
    2.Peel and finely slice the garlic(Fire)
    3.Add mix vegetables to hot dashi into a pot
    4.add chopped chicken(Earth)and simmer
    5.Add tablespoons of miso(Water)and turmeric(Wood)
    6.Garnish with chopped green onions(Metal)
Serve immediately

Method 2

---

1. Peel and cut the carrot(Metal)into thin slices
   2. Peel and cut taro(Wood)into pieces
   3. Add mix vegetables to hot dashi into a pot
   4. add chopped chicken(Earth)and simmer
   5. Add tablespoons of miso(Water)and konjac(Earth)
   6. Garnish with parsley(Fire)
   Serve immediately

Chrysanthemum

——————

Method 1

——————

1.Cut Chrysanthemum(Fire)into small pieces
  2.Soak shiitake mushrooms(Earth)in warm water,slice into
  bite-sized pieces
  3.Peel the carrots(Metal)and cut into strips
  4.Add mix vegetables to hot dashi into a pot and simmer
  5.Add tablespoons of miso(Water)
  6.Garnish with sesame seeds(Wood)
  Serve immediately

Method 2

1.Cut Chrysanthemum(Fire)into small pieces
   2.Cut block of tofu(Earth) into cubes
   3.Cut daikon(Wood)into bite-sized pieces
   4.Add mix vegetables to hot dashi into a pot and simmer
   5.Add tablespoons of miso(Water)and half a block of
cubed tofu
   6.Garnish with chopped green onions(Metal)
Serve immediately

Cucumber

_____

Method 1

_____

1.Cut cucumbers(Fire)thick into round slice.
    2.Peel the carrots(Metal)and cut into strips
    3.Cut block of tofu(Earth)into cubes
    4.Add mix vegetables to hot dashi into a pot and simmer
    5.Add tablespoons of miso(Water)and half a block of cubed tofu
    6.Garnish with the sesame seeds(Wood)
Serve immediately

Method 2

_____

1.Cut cucumbers(Fire)thick into round slice
    2.Peel and cut potatoes(Earth)into half round slices
    3.Cut daikon(Wood)into bite-sized pieces
    4.Add mix vegetables to hot dashi into a pot and simmer
    5.Add tablespoons of miso(Water)
    6.Garnish with chopped green onion(Metal)
Serve immediately

Eggplant

_____

Method 1

_____

1.Cut the eggplant(Earth)into bite-sized pieces
    2.Peel and finely slice the garlic(Fire)
    3.Peel the carrots(Metal)and cut into strips
    4.Add mix vegetables to hot dashi into a pot and simmer
    5.Add tablespoons of miso(Water)
    6.Garnish sesame seeds(Wood)
    Serve immediately

_____

Method 2

_____

1.Cut the eggplant(Earth)into bite-sized pieces
    2.Peel and finely slice the garlic(Fire)
    3.Peel and slice large tomato(Wood)
    4.Add mix vegetables to hot dashi into a pot simmer
    5.Add tablespoons of miso(Water)
    6.Garnish with chopped green onion(Metal)
    Serve immediately

Hijiki seaweed

_____

Method 1

_____

1.Wash Hijiki seaweed(Water)in warm water
    2.Cut block of tofu(Earth)into cubes
    3.Peel the carrots(Metal)and cut into strips
    4.Add mix vegetables to hot dashi into a pot and simmer
    5.Add tablespoons of miso(Water),half a block of cubed
tofu, and chopped ginger(Fire)
    6.Garnish with sesame seeds(Wood)
Serve immediately

_____

Method 2

_____

1.Wash Hijiki seaweed(Water)in warm water
    2.Peel and slice the burdock root(Fire)into pieces
    3.Cut fennel root(Wood)into bite-sized pieces
    4.Add mix vegetables to hot dashi into a pot and simmer
    5.Add tablespoons of miso(Water)and red beans(Earth)
    6.Garnish with chopped green onions(Metal)
Serve immediately

Kombu seaweed

———

Method 1

———

1. Wash Kombu seaweed(Water)in warm water
    2. Wash and half pumpkin(Earth),removing seeds and inner membrane,slice into large pieces
    3. Peel and cut the carrot(Metal)into thin slices
    4. Add mix vegetables to hot dashi into a pot and simmer
    5. Add tablespoons of miso(Water)and chopped ginger(Fire)
    6. Garnish with sesame seeds(Wood)
    Serve immediately

———

Method 2

———

1. Wash Kombu seaweed(Water)in warm water
    2. Soak shiitake mushrooms(Earth)in warm water,slice into bite-sized pieces
    3. Peel and cut the carrot(Metal)into thin slices
    4. Add mix vegetables to hot dashi into a pot and simmer
    5. Add tablespoons of miso(Water)and chopped ginger(Fire)
    6. Garnish with sesame seeds(Wood)
    Serve immediately

Kudzu

Method 1

1.Slice kudzu(Wood)into into thin slices
  2.Cut block of tofu(Earth)into cubes
  3.Peel and cut the carrot(Metal)into thin slices
  4.Simmer mix vegetables into a pot.Add miso(Water)
  5.Garnish with parsley(Fire)
  Serve immediately

Method 2

1.Slice kudzu(Wood)into thin slices
  2.Soak shiitake mushrooms(Earth)in warm water,slice into
  bite-sized pieces
  3.Peel and slice the burdock root(Fire)into pieces
  4.Add mix vegetables to hot dashi into a pot and simmer
  5.Add tablespoons of miso(Water)
  6.Garnish with chopped green onions(Metal)
  Serve immediately

Lotus root

_____

Method 1

_____

1. Wash and peel the lotus root(Earth),slice the lotus
   root into into round slice
   2. Cut fennel root(Wood)into bite-sized pieces
   3. Peel and cut the carrot(Metal)into thin slices
   4. Add mix vegetables to hot dashi into a pot and simmer
   5. Add tablespoons of miso(Water)
   6. Garnish with parsley(Fire)
   Serve immediately

Method 2

---

1. Wash and peel the lotus root(Earth),slice the lotus
   root into into round slice
   2. Peel and cut taro(Wood)into pieces
   3. Peel and cut the carrot(Metal)into thin slices
   4. Add mix vegetables to hot dashi into a pot and simmer
   5. Add tablespoons of miso(Water)
   6. Garnish with parsley(Fire)
   Serve immediately

Longan

_____

Method 1

_____

1.Peel and cut potatoes(Earth)into half round slices
   2.Cut fennel root(Wood)into bite-sized pieces
   3.Peel and cut the carrot(Metal)into thin slices
   4.Add mix vegetables to hot dashi into a pot and simmer
   5.Add tablespoons of miso(Water)and dried longan(Earth)
   6.Garnish with chopped green onions(Metal)
Serve immediately

_____

Method 2

_____

1.Wash and half pumpkin(Earth),slice into large pieces. Peel and cut the carrot(Metal
   2.Peel and finely slice shallots(Fire)
   3.Add mix vegetables to hot dashi into a pot and simmer
   4.Add tablespoons of miso(Water)and dried longan(Earth)
   5.Garnish with sesame seeds(Wood)
Serve immediately

Mugwort

————

Method 1

————

1.Chop the mugwort leaves(Fire) very finely
   2.Soak Shiitake mushrooms(Earth)in warm water,slice into
   bite-sized pieces
   3.Add mugwort leaves to hot dashi into a pot and simmer
   4.Add tablespoons of miso(Water)and shiitake mushrooms
   5.Add tablespoons of turmeric(Wood) and chopped
   ginger(Fire)
   6.Garnish with chopped green onions(Metal)
   Serve immediately

————

Method 2

————

1.Chop the mugwort leaves(Fire) very finely
   2.Cut block of tofu(Earth) into cubes
   3.Add tablespoons of miso(Water)and half a block of
   cubed tofu
   4.Add tablespoons of turmeric(Wood) and chopped
   ginger(Fire)
   5.Garnish with chopped green onions(Metal)
   Serve immediately

Okra

_____

Method 1

_____

1.Chop fresh okra(Earth)into slices
    2.Peel and slice large tomato(Wood)
    3.Peel the carrots(Metal)and cut into strips
    4.Add mix vegetables to hot dashi into a pot and simmer
    5.Add tablespoons of miso(Water)
    6.Garnish with parsley(Fire)
Serve immediately

_____

Method 2

_____

1.Chop fresh okra into slices(Earth)
    2.Wash Kombu seaweed(Water)in warm water
    3.Peel and cut the carrot(Metal)into thin slices
    4.Add tablespoons of miso(Water)and chopped ginger(Fire)
    5.Garnish with sesame seeds(Wood)
Serve immediately

Papaya

————

Method 1

————

1.Peel,seed,cut papaya(Earth)into small pieces
    2.Peel and cut the carrot(Metal)into thin slices
    3.Peel and slice the burdock root(Fire)into pieces
    4.Add mix vegetables to hot dashi into a pot and simmer
    5.Add tablespoons of miso(Water)
    6.Garnish with sesame seeds(Wood)
    Serve immediately

————

Method 2

————

1.Peel,seed,cut papaya(Earth)into small pieces
    2.Peel and slice large tomato(Wood)
    3.Peel and cut the carrot(Metal)into thin slices
    4.Add mix vegetables to hot dashi into a pot and simmer
    5.Add tablespoons of miso(Water)
    6.Garnish with parsley(Fire)
    Serve immediately

Pear

_____

Method 1

_____

1.Remove seeds and cut Asian pear(Earth)into large bite
    sizes
    2.Peel and cut the carrot(Metal)into thin slices
    3.Peel and finely slice shallots(Fire)
    4.Add mix vegetables to hot dashi into a pot and simmer
    5.Add tablespoons of miso(Water)and Asian pear
    6.Garnish with sesame seeds(Wood)
    Serve immediately

_____

Method 2

_____

1.Remove seeds and cut Asian pear(Earth)into large bite
    sizes
    2.Peel and cut taro(Wood)into pieces
    3.Peel and cut the carrot(Metal)into thin slices
    4.Add mix vegetables to hot dashi into a pot and simmer
    5.Add tablespoons of miso(Water)and Asian pear
    6.Garnish with parsley(Fire)
    Serve immediately

Peanuts

_____

Method 1

_____

1.Peel and cut the carrot(Metal)into thin slices
   2.Peel and finely slice the garlic(Fire)
   3.Add mix vegetables to hot dashi into a pot and simmer
   4.Add tablespoons of miso(Water)
   5.Add the peanuts(Earth)and chopped ginger(Fire)
   6.Garnish with sesame seeds(Wood)
Serve immediately

_____

Method 2

_____

1.Cut fennel root(Wood)into bite-sized pieces
   2.Peel and cut the carrot(Metal)into thin slices
   3.Add mix vegetables to hot dashi into a pot and simmer
   4.Add tablespoons of miso(Water)
   5.Add the peanuts(Earth)and red beans(Earth)
   6.Garnish with parsley(Fire)
Serve immediately

Potatoes

_____

Method 1

_____

1.Peel and cut potatoes(Earth)into half round slices
    2.Peel and slice large tomato(Wood)
    3.Peel and cut the carrot(Metal) into thin slices
    4.Add mix vegetables to hot dashi into a pot and simmer
    5.Add tablespoons of miso(Water)
    6.Garnish with parsley(Fire)
    Serve immediately

Method 2

———————

1.Peel and cut potatoes(Earth)into half round slices
  2.Cut fennel root(Wood)into bite-sized pieces
  3.Peel and cut the carrot(Metal)into thin slices
  4.Add mix vegetables to hot dashi into a pot and simmer
  5.Add tablespoons of miso(Water)
  6.Garnish with parsley(Fire)
  Serve immediately

Pumpkin

_____

Method 1

_____

1.Chop the pumpkin(Earth) into chunks
   2.Cut fennel root(Wood)into bite-sized pieces
   3.Peel and finely slice the garlic(Fire)
   4.Add mix vegetables to hot dashi into a pot and simmer
   5.Add tablespoons of miso(Water)
   6.Garnish with chopped green onions(Metal)
   Serve immediately

_____

Method 2

_____

1.Wash and half pumpkin(Earth),removing seeds and inner
   membrane,slice into large pieces
   2.Peel and cut the carrot(Metal)into thin slices
   3.Peel and slice the burdock root(Fire)into pieces
   4.Add mix vegetables to hot dashi into a pot and simmer
   5.Add tablespoons of miso(Water)
   6.Garnish with sesame seeds(Wood)
   Serve immediately

Read Beans

_____

Method 1

_____

1. Peel and cut potatoes(Earth) into half round slices
    2. Cut fennel root(Wood)into bite-sized pieces
    3. Peel and finely slice the garlic(Fire)
    4. Add mix vegetables to hot dashi into a pot and simmer
    5. Add tablespoons of miso(Water)and red beans(Earth)
    6. Garnish with chopped green onion(Metal)
    Serve immediately

_____

Method 2

_____

1. Wash Kombu seaweed(Water)in warm water
    2. Peel and finely slice the garlic(Fire)
    3. Peel and cut the carrot(Metal) into thin slices
    4. Add mix vegetables to hot dashi into a pot and simmer
    5. Add tablespoons of miso(Water)and red beans(Earth)
    6. Garnish with sesame seeds(Wood)
    Serve immediately

Rice

Method 1

1.Peel and cut taro(Wood)into pieces
   2.Peel and cut the carrot(Metal)into thin slices
   3.Add mix vegetables to hot dashi into a pot
   4.Add tablespoons of miso(Water)and chopped ginger(Fire)
   5.Add rice(Earth) and simmer
   6.Garnish with parsley(Fire)
   Serve immediately

Method 2

————

1.Peel and finely slice shallots(Fire)
   2.Peel and finely slice the garlic(Fire)
   3.Add mix vegetables to hot dashi into a pot
   4.Add tablespoons of miso(Water)and and red beans(Earth)
   5.Add rice(Earth)and simmer
   6.Garnish with sesame seeds(Wood)
   Serve immediately

Spinach

Method 1

1.Cut the spinach(Earth)into pieces
    2.Peel and slice the burdock root(Fire)into pieces
    3.Peel and cut the carrot(Metal)into thin slices
    4.Add mix vegetables to hot dashi into a pot and simmer
    5.Add tablespoons of miso(Water)
    6.Garnish with sesame seeds(Wood)
    Serve immediately

Method 2

1.Cut the spinach(Earth)into pieces
    2.Cut daikon(Wood)into bite-sized pieces
    3.Peel and finely slice the garlic(Fire)
    4.Add mix vegetables to hot dashi into a pot and simmer
    5.Add tablespoons of miso(Water)
    6.Garnish with chopped green onions(Metal)
    Serve immediately

Taro

_____

Method 1

_____

1.Peel and cut taro(Wood)into pieces
   2.Cut the spinach(Earth)into pieces
   3.Peel and slice the burdock root(Fire)into pieces
   4.Add mix vegetables to hot dashi into a pot and simmer
   5.Add tablespoons of miso(Water)
   6.garnish with chopped green onions(Metal)
   Serve immediately

_____

Method 2

_____

1.Peel and cut taro(Wood)into pieces
   2.Soak Shiitake mushrooms(Earth)in warm water,slice into
   bite-sized pieces
   3.Peel and cut the carrot(Metal)into thin slices
   4.Add mix vegetables to hot dashi into a pot and simmer
   5.Add tablespoons of miso(Water)
   6.Garnish with parsley(Fire)
   Serve immediately

Tomato

Method 1

1.Peel and slice large tomato(Wood)
   2.Cut and finely slice green pepper(Earth)
   3.Peel and finely slice shallots(Fire)
   4.Add mix vegetables to hot dashi into a pot and simmer
   5.Add tablespoons of miso(Water)
   6.Garnish with sesame seeds(Wood)
   Serve immediately

Method 2

1.Peel and slice large tomato(Wood)
2.Peel the carrots(Metal)and cut into strips
3.Soak Shiitake mushrooms(Earth)in warm water,slice into
bite-sized pieces
4.Add mix vegetables to hot dashi into a pot and simmer
5.Add tablespoons of miso(Water)
6.Garnish with parsley(Fire)
Serve immediately

Winter Melon

Method 1

1.Rinse winter melon(Earth) and cut into pieces
   2.Peel and cut taro(Wood)into pieces
   3.Peel and cut the carrot(Metal) into thin slices
   4.Add mix vegetables to hot dashi into a pot and simmer
   5.Add tablespoons of miso(Water)
   6.Garnish with parsley(Fire)
Serve immediately

Method 2

1.Rinse winter melon(Earth)and cut into pieces
   2.Peel the carrots(Metal)and cut into strips
   3.Slice shallot(Fire)thinly
   4.Add mix vegetables to hot dashi into a pot and simmer
   5.Add tablespoons of miso(Water)
   6.Garnish with sesame seeds(Wood)
Serve immediately

DIET PLAN

Monday

Breakfast - cooked rice,jasmine tea
Snack - edamame,raw vegetables
Lunch - cooked rice,carrot and bitter melon,jasmine tea
Snack - edamame,raw vegetables
Dinner - tofu, cooked rice,papaya,jasmine tea

Tuesday

Breakfast - soy,jasmine tea
Snack - edamame, raw vegetables
Lunch- grilled fish,jasmine tea
Snack - edamame, raw vegetables
Dinner- tofu,cooked rice,fuchiba,jasmine tea

Wednesday

Breakfast – tofu, jasmine tea
Snack – edamame,raw vegetables
Lunch- vegetable soup,cooked rice,jasmine tea
Snack – edamame,raw vegetables
Dinner- bitter melon,cooked rice,jasmine tea

Thursday

Breakfast - miso soup,jasmine tea
Snack - edamame,raw vegetables
Lunch - stir-fry vegetables,jasmin tea
Snack - edamame,raw vegetables
Dinner- tofu,sweet potato soup,jasmine tea

Friday

Breakfast - spinach,jasmine tea
Snack - edamame,raw vegetables
Lunch- pork,jasmine tea
Snack - edamame,raw vegetables
Dinner- wakame,fruit,jasmine tea

Saturday

Breakfast- cooked rice, jasmine tea
Snack - edamame,raw vegetables
Lunch- soba noodle,jasmine tea
Snack - edamame,raw vegetables
Dinner- goya, jasmine tea

Sunday

Breakfast- miso soup,jasmine tea
Snack – eedamame,raw vegetables
Lunch – baked sweet potatoes,jasmine tea
Snack – eedamame,raw vegetables
Dinner- Shiitake,jasmine tea

RYUKYU CUISINE

The prefecture of Okinawa at the south of Japan once flourished as the independent Ryukyu Dynasty through trade with China, and the traditions of the Ryukyu Dynasty live in the modern Ryukyu cuisine today.

The kingdom established the tradition of Ryukyuan palace cuisine. for visiting Chinese envoys of the Ming dynasty and foreign dignitaries of other Asian countries as a way of demonstrating hospitality,while sharing Okinawa's food culture with the world.

Recipes

Andagi - Okinawan Donuts.

Ingredients:cake flour,egg,brown sugar,baking powder,canola oil.

Directions:

1.Break the egg into a bowl and beat it. Add the sugar and mix well.

2.Add the canola oil,cake flour and baking powder

4.Roll the dough into sized balls.Deep fry the dough balls slowly.

————

Asa jiru - soup seasoned with of asa seaweed.

Ingredients:dry asa,tofu, bonito-based dashi,soy sauce.

Directions:

————

1. Soak asa in cold water and wash.

2. Bring bonito soup to boil.Mix Chopped tofu in the soup with asa. and soy sauce to taste.

Bell Pepper Champuru
Ingredients:green bell peppers,sliced pork,eggs,bonito-based dashi broth,canoil oil.
Directions:
1.Cut the bell peppers into thin strips. Cut pork into bite-sized pieces.
2.Stir-fry pork in a frying pan.Add the bell pepper and the dashi stock granules.
3.Swirl in the beaten eggs and mix.

_____

Beniimo – steamed purple sweet potato

_____

Ingredients: purple sweet potato, cake flour, baking powder, egg butter.

_____

Directions:

_____

1. Peel the skin off the purple sweet potato and cut into
   small cubes.
2. Break and Beat an egg in a bowl.Mix sugar, butter,flour and baking powder into the bowl.
3.Add sweet potatoes, then mix gently.
4. Pour the mixture into cups. Place the cups in a steam cooker.

Boroboro juushii – mugwort,soup.

Ingredients:onion, canola oil,bonito-based dashi broth,potato,mugwort leaves,milk

----

Directions:

1.Sauté the onion in canola oil.
  2.Add the dashi brothpo and tato pieces,
  3.Add chopped mugwort leaves and the milk, and simmer.

Bira-garamachi –s squid tube.
  Ingredients:green onions,squid tube,vinegar,white sesame seeds, awamori sake, bonito-based dashi broth.

Directions:
  1.Aboil the green onions.
  2.Boil the squid. Cut it into strips.
  3.Wrap the green onions around the squid strips.
  4.Add white sesame seeds, awamori sake,dashi broth and mix thoroughly.
  5.Serve with the vinegar-poured over top.

Carrot Shirishiri
Ingredients: carrot,eggs,bonito-based dashi broth,canola oil
Directions:
1.Peel the carrot, cut it into thin strips.
2.Sauté the carrot in a frying pan with canola oil.
3.Beat the eggs and mix in dashi stock.
4.Mix carrots in the beaten eggs.

———————

Chicken Karaage – style deep fried chicken.
Ingredients:soy sauce, awamori sake,mirin ginger grated,garlic,potato starch,canola oil.
Directions:
1.Cut chicken thigh into pieces. Marinate it in the plastic bag with all the other ingredients.
2.Roll pieces of chicken in potato starch.
3.Drop chicken into the hot oil.

Chimushinji – Okinawan pork and vegetable soup
Ingredients:pork liver,shimaninjin carrots,green onion,soy sauce
Directions:
1. Cut pork liver into bite size pieces.
2. Slice shimaninjin and green onion.
3. Boil pork liver, and shimaninjin in a pot.
4. Add green onion and soy sauce.

Chinsuko – Okinawan Cookies.
Ingredients:flour,sugar,pure lard
Directions:
1.Preheat oven to 150 degrees.Mix pure lard and sugar.
2.Add flour also little by little.Bake for 25 minutes.

Duruwakashii – taimo sweet potato.

Ingredients:small taimo,pork,kamaboko fish paste,dried shiitake mushrooms,bonito-based dashi broth.

Directions:

1. Peel taimo and slice. Soak dry mushrooms in cold water.

3.Chop pork, fish paste, and into small cubes.

4.Boil dry mushroom andtaimo slices,let simmer.

5.Add kamaboko fish paste and serve.

Fu Chanpuru-fried mix vegetables.
Ingredients: eggs, awamori sake, soy sauce,chinese chives,canola oil
Directions:
1.Beat the eggs and stir in the soy sauce and awamori.
2.Chop the Chinese chives into pieces.
3.Heat a frying pan,place egg mixture
4.Add the Chinese chives and and serve.

Gōyā champuru - fried mix vegetables with pork.
Ingredients:bittermelon,pork,tofu,eggs,bonito flakes, awamori sake,soy sauce,bonito-based dashi broth,canola oil
Directions:
1.Slice the bitter melon and tofu.Coat the pork in flour.
2.Saute the the cubes tofu in a pan.
3.Add canola oil and stir fry the pork..Add the bitter melon.
4.Add the bonito flakes, in the beaten eggs.

———

Gyoza - dumplings.
Ingredients:ground pork,myoga ginger,shiso leaves,umeboshi plum,canola oil,flour, vinegar,soy sauce.
Directions:
1.Chop the myoga.
2.Tear the shiso leaves into pieces.
3.Add myoga, umeboshi, and shiso leaves to the pork
4.Fry the gyoza dumplings on the pan
5.Pour the flour and water together into the pan.
6.Serve with rice vinegar mixed with soy sauce.

Gyu-don – sweet and salty beef with rice.

Ingredients:sliced beef plate,onion,dried shiitake mushrooms, ginger,awamori sake ,soy sauce,canola oil,steamed rice.

———

Directions:

1.Cook sliced beef in canola oil untill the beef's color changes.

2. Add mushrooms,onion and ginger with the beef.

3. Dish up the rice into a bowl, add the cooked beef. With the soy sauce on top.

Gurugun karaage - deep-fried fly fish.
Ingredients:gurukuma,onion, carrot, potato starch,soy sauce,awamori sake.
Directions:
1.Cut the fish into bite size pieces. Dust the fish with potato starch.
2.Cook the fish in a pan until the fish becomes a little golden in color.Add sliced onion and carrot.
3. Pour soy sauce,sake on top. Put in a refrigerator and serve.

Handama - salad of local vegetables

_____

Ingredients:Handama,leaf lettuce,bell peppers,boiled eggs

_____

Directions:

_____

1.Cut Handama leaves and the lettuce into bite size portions. Drain water from the vegetables.
  2.Place vegetables in a bowl, add boiled eggs and dressing on the top.

Hirayāchii- Okinawan pancake

Ingredients:flour,egg,water,bonito flakes.canola oil.

Directions:
1. Mix the cake flour, water in a bowl and mix well.
2. Heat a pan and pour some canola oil.
3. Pour flour mix into the pan and sprinkle the bonito flakes.

Hijiki Gohan – steamed rice with hijiki seaweed.

Ingredients:Hijiki seaweed, rice,carrot,soy sauce,awamori sake,bonito-based dashi broth.

Directions:

---

1. Shred the carrot.
   2. Boil the rice in a saucepan. Add carrot, hijiki seaweed , soy sauce and awamori sake.

Horenso no shiroae – Steamed spinach.

––––––––––

Ingredients:blanches of spinach, white sesame seeds,block tofu,soy sauce.
    Directions:
    1.Boil the spinach in a saucepan.
    2.Mix white sesame, tofu,soy sauce in a bowl. Add the spinach.

Inamuruchi miso – local soup cooked for celebrations.

––––––––––

Ingredients:pork belly,Kamaboko yellow boiled fish paste,konjac,miso.

––––––––––

Directions:

––––––––––

1.Cut konjac in thin slices.
    2.Boil the pork slices until soft.
    3.Add konjac and Kamaboko yellow boiled fish.
    4.Mix all ingredients.Add miso to taste.

Jyushi - steamed rice with mixed vegetables.

_____

Ingredients:rice pork belly,carrot,bonito-based dashi broth, soy sauce,awamori sake.

_____

Directions:
1.Boil the pork belly into a saucepan.
2.Slice the kelp ad the carrot into thin strips.
3.Boil the rice into saucepan. Add dashi broth.
4.Add soy sauce and sake.

Kaki furai - deep-fried oysters.

_____

Ingredients:oysters,eggs,panko breadcrumbs,leaves cabbage ,cucumber, carrot ,onion, parsley,lemon.

_____

Directions:
1. Dust the oysters with the flour
2. Dip them into the beaten egg, then coat them with the bread crumbs.
3. Cook oysters.Put all the garnish ingredients,and serve with the oysters and a lemon wedge.

_____

Kinpira Gobo - braised burdock.

_____

Ingredients:gobo burdock root,carrot,canola oil, white sesame seeds,Ichimi Togarashi chili pepper,bonito-based dashi broth,awamori sake,soy sauce

_____

Directions:
1. Slice gobo thinly into thin matchbox strips.
2. Cut carrots into matchbox strips.
3. In a frying pan, stir fry gobo. Add carrot,dashi,sake,soy sauce.
4. Sprinkle sesame seeds and Ichimi Togarashi chili pepper.

Kombu roll - swordfish wrapped in kombu seaweed.
Ingredients:dried kombu (kelp),soy sauce,sake.

————

Directions:

————

1.Cut swordfish into long strips.
   2.Place a strip of the swordfish on top of a sheet of kombu and roll it.
   3.Boil kombu rolls in a medium pot.
   4.Add sugar, sake, soy sauce to the pot.

Kuubu irichi - braised kombu and pork.

———

Ingredients:dried kelp, pork belly,carrot, canola oil,awamori sake,soy sauce,bonito-based dashi broth.

———

Directions:

———

1.Cook the pork in a saucepan.Once the pork changes color, add sake.
   2. Add kelp, carrot and and dashi, soy sauce. Mix all the ingredients gently.

**Maaminaa Champuru - ** fried bean sprouts.
Ingredients:bean sprouts, carrot, pork, tofu,bonito-based dashi broth,soy sauce.

———————

Directions:

———————

1. Cut the carrot, bean sprouts and tofu
   2.Cook the pork into a pan.Add the carrot,bean sprouts and dashi stock.
   3.Add tofu and soy sauce and mix all ingredients.

Maasuni – traditional Okinawan fish simmered in salt.
Ingredients:white fish,ocean salt, awamori sake,parsley.
Directions:
1. boil water,salt and awamori in a pan .
2. Add the fish and cook on medium heat.Add and parsley.

Mimigaa- pigs' ears boiled.

————————

Ingredients:pig's ears, onion,carrots,parsley.

————————

Directions:
    1.Boil the ears in a large pot.
    2.Add the rest of the ingredients.
    3.Cut the ears into slivers, then fry in a wok.

Minudaru - pork marinated.

————

Ingredients:pork loin,brown sugar,soy sauce, awamori, sesame seeds, ginger.

————

Directions:

————

1.Mix together the brown sugar,soy sauce,and awamori.
    2.Add the marinade to the ground sesame seeds.Place it to the top of pork .
    3.Steam the pork over medium heat.Cut into pieces, and serve with ginger.

Mochi – mochi soup eaten around New Year.

_____

Ingredients:daikon radish,carrot,shiitake mushrooms,h,soy sauce,spinach, mochi rice cakes.

_____

Directions:

_____

1. Cut daikon into slices. Cut the carrot into long diagonal slices.Cut the spinach into pieces.
   2.Boil the daikon radish, carrot,and shiitake mushrooms in a pot.
   3.Grill the mochi mochi rice.Combine the ingredients and heat.

Moui – marinated Okinawan yellow cucumber.
Ingredients:yellow cucumber,ocean salt, dried bonito flakes.
Directions:
1.Slice the moui and cucumber thin.
2.Put the slices in a plastic bag, and add salt.
3.Serve garnished with dried bonito flakes.

Mozuku Soup - mozuku seaweed soup.
Ingredients:okra, mozuku seaweed,eggs,bonito-based dashi broth.

————————

Directions:
1.Wash mozuku seaweed and cut into small slices.
2.Let boil dashi broth. Add mozuku and the eggs.

Naabeera Soup -cucumber soup.
Ingredients:cucumber,tofu,pork hash, bonito-based dashi broth,miso.

Directions:
1.Peel cucumbers and cut into round slice.
2.Boil sliced cucumber until tender in a pan, and add dashi broth.
3.Add pork hash,tofu and miso to a pan.

Nakami jiru - pork guts soup.

––––––––

Ingredients:pork guts,pork,kamaboko fish paste,konnyaku , bonito-based dashi broth,soy sauce,ginger, wheat flour.

––––––––

Directions:

––––––––

1.Cut kamaboko, and pork into strips.
   2.Boil the pork guts in the pot. Sprinkle wheat flour over
   3.In a saucepan, boil dashi broth.Add kamaboko,soy sauce and grated ginger.

Ohitashi – Boiled okra.

––––––––––

Ingredients:okra,dried bonito flakes,soy sauce,ocean salt.

––––––––––

Directions:
1. Sprinkle ocean salt on cut Okra.
2. Boil Okra and chop into slices.
3. Sprinkle over with dried bonito and add soy sauce.

Papaya Champuru
Ingredients:papaya,carrot,green peppers,chinese chives, bonito-based dashi broth,soy sauce.
Directions:
1.Cut the papaya, carrots, chinese chives and the green pepper into thin strips.
2.Stir-fry the green pepper and carrot.
3.Add the papaya and the Chinese chives.
4.Add the bonito-based dashi stock granules and soy sauce

————————

PO-PO Crepes - Okinawan dessert.
Ingredients: flour, baking powder, eggs, salt, miso,batter.

————————

Directions:
1.Beat eggs and water,add flour, salt, baking powder.
2.Heat a pan,add batter,pour all ingredients.
3.Spread miso filling and roll into cylinders.

Rafute - braised pork belly.

Ingredients: pork loin,soy sauce,awamori sake,sesame seeds
   Directions:
   1.Mix together the brown sugar, salt,soy sauce, and awamori.
   2.Cut the pork into slices, place in the mix to marinate.
   3.Cut the pork into easy-to-eat pieces
   4.Sprinkle with Sesame seeds.Serve on a plate.

Renkon – lotus root salad.
   Ingredients: lotus roots, mushrooms,oil, salt
   Directions:
   1.Heat canola oil in a pan and add shiitake.
   2.Add lotus roots and salt.

Somen Champuru - noodles with stir fried vegetables.
Ingredients:somen noodles, carrot, onion,cabbage, bonito-based dashi broth.

Directions:
    1.Cut each vegetable to bite size.Boil somen noodles.
    2.Stir fry the cut vegetables in a pan. Season with bonito-based dashi broth.
    3.Mix everything with somen in a pan.

Shibui champuru – fried tougan winter melon.

————

Ingredients:winter melon, pork belly,ginger, bonito fish flakes,canola oil,white sesame.

————

Directions:

————

1. Cook the pork belly, ginger and the winter melon in a pan.
   2. Add bonito fish flakes and mix well.
   5. Place on a plate and sprinkle white sesame for garnish.

Soba – Okinawan noodle soup.
Ingredients:pork belly,soba noodles,green onion,awamori sake soy sauce,ginger.
Directions:
1.Place the pork belly into a pressure cooker pot.
2.Remove from heat and then cut it into slices.
3.Add soy sauce, and awamori sake.
4.Boil the noodles, and put them in bowls.
5.Serve topped with pork, ginger, and green onion.

―――――

Soki jiro - pork ribs soup.

―――――

Ingredients:pork ribs,flour,kombu kelp,burdock root,carrot,canola oil, soy sauce,awamori sake,bonito-based dashi broth.
Directions:
1.Cut the pork into pieces,coat the surface in the flour.
3.Deep-fry the pork until the surface turns a light golden brown.
4.In a pot, combine the dashi, soy sauce, and awamori, the fried pork until the simmering broth thickens.
5.Add the kombu kelp, burdock root and carrot
6.Arrange on a serving dish and serve.

Shima Rakkyo – salted scallions.
Ingredients:shima rakkyo,dried bonito flakes,ocean salt.

———————

Directions:
1.Cut shima rakkyo scallions
2.Put scallions and salt in a bag and shake. Add dried bonito flakes.

Taco-Rice – popular dish among U.S. military personnel stationed in Okinawa.

Ingredients:rice, minced beef,onion,lettuce,tomatoes, ketchup,cheese.

Directions:

1.Heat the chopped onion on a pan. Add minced meat and ketchup.

2.Place rice on a plate.Add lettuce, cheese and fresh tomatoes on top.

Tako - octopus carpaccio.

————

Ingredients:octopus tentacle,onion,canola oil,lemon juice,garlic, salt,parsley
Directions:
1.Slice the onion,octopus, into bite size pieces.
2.Combine dressing ingredients.
3.Serve on plate and pour dressing on.

Tebichi - boiled pig's feet.

Ingredients:pig's feet,kombu, dried shiitake mushrooms,daikon (turnip),soy sauce,awamori sake, parsley.

Directions:

1.Boil pig's feet,then add ginger.
   2.Add kombu, mushrooms and daikon.
   3.Add soy sauce and sake, cover and simmer.
   4.Serve with parsley.

Tempura - portuguese dish consisting of vegetables that have been deep fried.
Ingredients:kakiage vegetables dipped in batter,flour,canola oil.
Directions:
1.Place the shrimp in a bowl, then add the cut mitsuba.
2.Sprinkle on the flour,then mix in the water.
3.Heat oil ,place battered mixture to the heated oil.
4.Turn the mixture over once again, remove from the oil and serve.

Tofu champuru - tofu stir-fried.

Ingredients: tofu,onion,Chinese chives, bonito flakes,awamori sake,canola oil,soy sauce.

Directions:

1.Boil the tofu, pour into a strainer and drain.

2.Cut the onion slices and Chinese chives.

3.Stir-fry the tofu in a frying pan. Add the onions,awamori sake and soy sauce.

4.Add bonito flakes and the Chinese chives.

Tonjiru – pork miso soup.
Ingredients:pork belly,daikon radish,carrot,burdock root,konnyaku, green onion,kombu,soy sauce.
Directions:
1.Cut the pork into pieces.
2.Cut the daikon radish, carrot, burdock root, green onion and konnyaku into long, narrow slices.
3.Fry the pork in the pot.Add the daikon radish,carrot, burdock root, konnyaku.
4.Add the water,kombu and bring to a boil.
5.Add the soy sauce, green onion and serve.

———————

Tsukemono - pickled cucumber sunomono
Ingredients:cucumbers,vinegar,canola oil,brown sugar,ocean salt.
Directions:
1.Wash the and cut cucumbers.
2.Mix all ingredients in a plastic bag, leave for one hour.

Unagi – eel grilled.
Ingredients:eel,cooked rice,soy sauce.
Directions:
1.Cut the eel meat into two fillets.
2.Place unagi over a grill, turning over until the entire skin side has browned.
3.Dip unagi in the soy sauce.Place over top of the rice.

————

Urizun - marinated beans.
Ingredients:beans,bonito flakes
Directions:
1.Boil the Urizun beans in the pan
2.Mix with Bonito flakes

————

Yakitori -Barbecued chicken on skewer.
Ingredients: chicken breasts, soy sauce,awamori sake, sugar.
Directions:
1.Boil all ingredients in a pan for sauce
2.Barbeque the chicken pieces.
3.Coat chicken with sauce.

KAMPO THERAPY

Kampo medicine emphasize the characteristics of whole foods, based on the concept of balancing the *Yin* (cold) and the *Yang* (warm).This balance is integral to understanding Okinawa diet as well as for the maintenance of good health.

Meat

Beef	Warm	Sweet
Chicken	Warm	Sweet
Goat meat	Warm	Sweet
Pork	Neutral	Sweet, salty

Dairy Products

Butter	Cool	Sweet, fatty
Cheese goat	Warm	Acrid, salty, sweet
Chicken egg	Neutral	Sweet

Fish and Seafood

Crab	Cold	Sweet, salty
Eel	Warm	Sweet
Mackerel	Warm	Sweet
Lobster	Neutral	Sweet, salty
Mussel	Warm	Salty
Octopus	Neutral	Sweet, salty
Oyster	Neutral	Sweet, salty
Sardine	Warm	Sweet, salty
Shrimp	Warm	Sweet
tuna	Neutral	Sweet
Squid	Neutral	Salty, sweet

Legumes

Aduki bean	Neutral	Sweet, sour
Natto	Warm	Sweet
Endomame	Neutral	Sweet
Soybean	Neutral	Sweet
Tofu	Cool	Sweet

Graines

Rice, brown	Warm		Sweet
Mochi rice	Warm		Sweet, bitter
Wheat	Cool		Sweet

Seeds

Lotus seed	Neutral	Sweet, astringent
Pumpkin seed	Warm	Sweet
Sesame	Neutral	Sweet

Flavourlings

Miso $\quad$ C $\quad$ S
old $\quad$ alty

Soy $\quad$ C $\quad$ S
sauce $\quad$ ool $\quad$ alty

Sugar $\quad$ W $\quad$ S
arm $\quad$ weet

Spices and Herbs

Garlic	Warm	Acrid
Ginger	Warm	Acrid
Mugwort	Warm	Bitter, acrid
Mustard Seeds	Warm	Acrid
Myoga ginger	Cold	Bitter, sweet
Salt	Cold	Salty
Pepper sansho	Hot	Acrid
Turmeric	Warm	Acrid, bitter
Wasabi	Warm	Acrid

Mushrooms

Shii Ne S
take utral weet

Seaweeds

Hijiki   C   S
          old   alty

Kelp   C   S
kombu   old   alty

Vegetables

Alfalfa sprouts	Cool	Bitter
Artichoke	Cool	Bitter, sweet
Asparagus	Cold	Sweet, bitter
Bamboo Shoots	Cold	Sweet
Bitter melon	Cold	Sweet, bitter
Broccoli	Neutral	Sweet
Burdock root	Cool	Acrid, bitter
Cabbage	Neutral	Sweet, bitter
Carrot	Neutral	Sweet, acrid
Cauliflower	Neutral	Sweet, bitter
Celery	Cool	Sweet, bitter
Chinese leek	Warm	Acrid
Cucumber	Cold	Sweet, bitter
Eggplant	Cool	Sweet
Green pepper	Neutral	Acrid, sweet
Parsley	Cool	Sweet
Konjac	Cool	Sweet
Leek	Warm	Acrid, sweet
Lettuce	Cool	Bitter, sweet
Lotus root	Neutral	Sweet, astringent
Mustard green	Warm	Acrid
Cabbage	cool	Sweet

181

Okra	Neutral	Bitter, sweet, slimy
Onion	Warm	Acrid, Sweet
Parsley	Warm	Acrid
Parsnip	Neutral	Sweet, bitter, acrid
Potato	Neutral	Sweet
Pumpkin	Warm	Sweet
Daikon	Cool	Acrid, sweet
Rakkyo	Warm	Acrid, bitter
green onion	Warm	Acrid
Shiso	Warm	Acrid
Soybean sprout	Cool	Sweet
Spinach	Cool	Sweet
Squash	Warm	Sweet
Sweet Potato	Neutral	Sweet
Taro	Neutral	Acrid
Tomato	Cool	Sweet, sour

Fruits

Avocado	Cool	Sweet
Banana	Cool	Sweet
Guava	Warm	Sweet, astringent
Lemon	Cool	Sour, astringent
Longan	Warm	Sweet
Loquat fruits	Neutral	Sweet, sour
Mango	Cool	Sweet, sour
Papaya	Neutral	Sweet, bitter
Passion fruit	Cool	Bitter, bland
Persimmon	Cold	Sweet, astringent
Pineapple	Neutral	Sweet, astringent
Ume Plum	Warm	Sour
Watermelon	Cold	Sweet

BEVERAGES

Beer	Cool	Bitter, sweet
Sake	Warm	Sweet, bitter
Green tea	Cold	Bitter, sweet, astringent
Jasmine tea	Warm	Acrid
Milk goat	Warm	Sweet

WEB SITES

Okinawa Centenarian Study:
   http://www.okicent.org

———

Center for Kampo Medicine:
   http://www.keio-kampo.jp/index_en.html

———

Okinawa Karate Kaikan:
   http://www.karatekaikan.jp

———

Uchinaanchu festival:
   http://wuf2016.com/en

———

The National Theatre Okinawa:
   http://www.nt-okinawa.or.jp/

———

National Museum of Etnology:
   http://www.minpaku.ac.jp/english/

———

Peace Memorial Museum:
   http://www.peace-museum.pref.okinawa.jp

———

Tourism Board
   http://www.visitokinawa.jp

RECOMMENDED READING

Willcox,Bradley J., D. Craig. Willcox, and Makoto Suzuki. The Okinawa Program: How the World's Longest-lived People Achieve Everlasting Health and How You Can Too. New York: Clarkson Potter,2001.

_____

Nagamine,Shoshin.The Essence of Okinawan Karate-Do:(Shorin-Ryu). Charles E Tuttle Co,1998.

_____

Clarke,Michael.The Art of Hojo Undo.YMAA Publication Center,2009.

_____

Sakihara,Mitsugu.Brief History of Early Okinawa Based on the Omoro Soshi.University of Hawaii Press,1987.

_____

Sered,Susan Starr.Women of the Sacred Groves:Divine Priestesses of Okinawa. Oxford Univ Press,1999.

_____

Nakasone,Ronald Y,Okinawan Diaspora.University of Hawaii Press,2002.

Acknowledgments

Special thank to my mother Alba who inspired me in the creation of this book. Big thanks to all my readers – whether you read and share in many ways than you could possibly know.

About the Author

Marco Carestia is an anthropologist specialized in Culture of Japan with training in Japan Consolate of Milan,on the basis of his Diploma of Japanese. He has focused his studies on food culture since Milan Expo 2015.

Stay in Touch

I'd greatly appreciate it if you could leave me a review at Amazon to help others discover it, so that they can benefit from the content as well.

May you enjoy real peace and happiness.

————

Media Contact

http://www.marcocarestia.it
http://www.marcocarestiasensory.com/
https://www.goodreads.com/author/show/16726707.Marco_Carestia

Kyoto

Visual anthropology methods include the use of images to stimulate culturally relevant reflections.Anthropologists are interested in how religious ideas express the role of humans within the world. Conceptually,all aspects of culture can be captured on photo without limitations.

The end results are photo essays which communicate visual aspects of reality. Similarly,visual anthropology find themselves involved with the research of image makers.

The beautiful thing about visual anthropology is images don't necessarily need to be technically perfect.The shooter can simply take an image to catch some form of interesting content,by capturing spontaneously the essence of a place and the people.

This is especially true for visual anthropology as getting close to subject is an important consideration to capture a culture manifested through visible. Pictures provide a source of symbols situated in constructed and natural environments.

This book is a must-have for any japan enthusiast, capturing the essential elements that distinguish Japanese culture. The work contains photos taken in various places in Kyoto , a place deeply influenced by the nature.

The Japan's ancient capital manifest a unique ability to meld the sensuality of nature with the discipline of meditation.Japan's ancient capital is the home of gardens and holy temples.

The beauty of city offers a wide variety of experiences and sights: you'll find ancient masterpieces of religious architecture.

To experience the essence of Kyoto, you must walk its unique districts. Kyoto ensure the most enriching and authentic experience and the photos taken on a photographic tour became the story of the most breathtaking locale site illustrated with vivid images .

The photobook brings to life the histories and aesthetics of japanese cultural heritage.At the heart of Kyoto is harmony with nature, simply a place of serenity and rest:one of the best reasons to immerse yourself in a completely Japanese spirituality.

This book is available on Amazon in a paperback and Kindle edition.

About the Author

V Marco Carestia is an anthropologist specialized in Culture of Japan with training in Japan Consolate of Milan,on the basis of his Diploma of Japanese.He has focused his studies on food culture since Milan Expo 2015.

    Read more at <u>Marco Carestia's site</u>.

Made in the USA
Columbia, SC
08 June 2022

61481181R00117